A Robust Think Tank for Africa

A Robust Think Tank for Africa

Words of Hope, Ingenuity and Faith

FRANCIS CHISHALA

PARTRIDGE
A Penguin Random House Company

Copyright © 2014 by Francis Chishala.

ISBN: Softcover   978-1-4828-0381-5
           eBook   978-1-4828-0380-8

All rights reserved. No part of this book may be used or reproduced in any manner whatsoever without written permission except in the case of brief quotations embodied in critical articles, reviews and for academic purposes. For information, address Partridge Africa Publishing, customersupport.africa@partridgepublishing.com or the author, chishfc@gmail.com

Scripture quotations are from The Revised Standard Version of the Bible: Catholic Edition, copyright © 1965, 1966 the Division of Christian Education of the National Council of the Churches of Christ in the United States of America. Used by permission. All rights reserved.

Because of the dynamic nature of the Internet, any web addresses or links contained in this book may have changed since publication and may no longer be valid. The views expressed in this work are solely those of the author and do not necessarily reflect the views of the publisher, and the publisher hereby disclaims any responsibility for them.

Print information available on the last page.

To order additional copies of this book, contact
Toll Free 0800 990 914 (South Africa)
+44 20 3014 3997 (outside South Africa)
orders.africa@partridgepublishing.com

www.partridgepublishing.com/africa

Contents

Dedication vii
Epigraph ix
Acknowledgement xi
Preface xiii
Prologue xv

Chapter One 1
    An Issue of Human Rights
Chapter Two 5
    Unpalatable Utterances
Chapter Three 8
    Communication in the workplace
Chapter Four 13
    Africa's Economic Emancipation
Chapter Five 17
    Respect the differences
Chapter Six 21
    The Culture of Silence
Chapter Seven 25
    The Press in a Democratic Africa
Chapter Eight 29
    The 'Za-yellow' Phenomenon
Chapter Nine 33
    Connected by a click
Chapter Ten 36
    ICT Power to the People
Chapter Eleven 39
    The Leader you can become

Chapter Twelve 42
    We Need a Robust African Think-Tank
Chapter Thirteen 46
    Oil Production and the future of Africa
Chapter Fourteen 51
    Arms Trafficking
Chapter Fifteen 62
    Models of a Free Media
Chapter Sixteen 65
    Story telling: Tell it like it is
Chapter Seventeen 68
    The Global Economic Recession and Africa
Chapter Eighteen 71
    The Nature of Travel Journalism
Chapter Nineteen 84
    Assessment Narrative
Chapter Twenty 89
    Communication and Human Understanding
Chapter Twenty One 93
    Media messages
Chapter Twenty-Two 101
    Zambia's Democracy and Development: Two Key Moments
Chapter Twenty-Three 113
    Africa and the Cinema of Revolution
Chapter Twenty-Four 118
    Rhetoric as an Aid to Modern Advertisement
Chapter Twenty-Five 121
    Parable of talents
Chapter Twenty-Six 129
    Forgiveness and Reconciliation
Chapter Twenty-Seven 135
    Jesus Christ with a Zambian Face
Chapter Twenty-Eight 141
    Christmas and Children

Work Referenced in this book 145

Dedication

For mum *Grace Chipili Chisembe*, a phenomenon woman who sacrificed and invested in my education and faith.

Epigraph

Though we speak much we cannot reach the end,
And the sum of our words is:
"He is the all." Sirach 43: 27.

Acknowledgement

This work would not have become a reality without the help of others. I feel indebted to my editors Frs. Jim McGloin, S.J. (Socius ZAM), William Bichl, S.J (Assistant Alumni Affairs at JCU Ohio) and Thomas Schubeck, S.J (Emeritus Professor of Theology at JCU Ohio) who read through part of the script and made the topographical and grammatical alterations. I am grateful to these companions also for the variable suggestions they made to the script. I owe much to my brother Jesuits I shared the community with during the period of writing these articles. Most of these companions who encouraged me to write lived with me in the following communities Mukasa Minor Seminary (2003-2005), Luwisha House (2008), Elms Jesuits (2005-2007), Ushirika (2008-2011) and most especially the warmth and support of the Schell House Jesuits (2015) where the idea to compile these articles into a book was born.

I thank the following Fathers: Gerry Karras, S.J, Pete Henriot, S.J, Orobator, S.J and Gabriel Massi, S.J, my one time superiors who would have read some of these articles in their earlier form for publication in the media and Jesuit reviews and Bulletins.

Special thanks to Mr. Tobias Milambo and Mrs Maluba Sikopo for providing part of the financial resources for the publishing of the book. I am indebted to my provincial Fr. Emmanuel Mumba, S.J and Province Treasurer Fr. Tadeusz Swiderski, S.J for buying into the project agreeing the province to finance the printing of the copies of the books.

Preface

Repetition and practice is the art of mastering and perfecting. Those who have done things better have always aligned themselves with those who have walked the road to learn from their experiences. *A Robust Think Tank for Africa,* is a culmination of brilliantly crafted pieces of writings for the print and online media indicating different genre in opinion, analysis and investigative journalism married with a collection of grade A essays in communication theories and how they apply to contemporary media. The four last chapters are dedicated to faith and social justice resonating with a principle in the Jesuit tradition of promoting a faith that does justice.

In this book I attempt to show case journalistic writings and analysis as a specialized reporter, essay writer, media analyst, opinion leader and believer by exposing you to my finest writings of over a decade. With this book in your hand, if you are a writer, you have a perfect tool kit to begin walking the talk and surely your passion for the word on paper will upsurge to excellence.

I have been told several times by those who read my work either academic or in the media that I write well and I know that myself. I have once won a national essay competition and sometimes received payment for my writings but it is not the extrinsic rewards that motivate me to write. Writing does not come easy for me either, sometimes I find myself putting my ideas down on paper because I believe there is something important I want to share with others. I want to teach, inspire and provoke thought in others. I write because I like to write and not because I must. No one holds a gun at me to write nor do I feel pressured to write. I simply write because I enjoy writing. It is my hobby. It takes days to perfect a piece according to required standards. Sometimes it is frustrating, but I love the experience and have passion for journalism. I want to write and teach others how to write. My best experiences have been in class when I teach journalism and public relations students on how to write essays and how to write effective sentences in English. It is for this reason the thought of jotting down *A Robust Think Tank for Africa,* for aspiring writers and those who have a heart for Africa was born.

My approach is that when I get an idea I jot it down then I think of how to develop it according to three main points. This helps me to focus and not try to say everything in a single essay. Focusing is very important. Research is important in developing new ideas. I research by sharing my ideas with friends and reading. I write down what I know on the subject. Once I have done this, I find my writings flow more smoothly. At other times I simply feel inspired and am in the right mood for writing. That comes after I have done some hard study and liked an idea. It also comes when I had witnessed an event and thought about it critically and sometimes when I got an insight in the middle of the night.

Writing can be fun but it requires discipline. I enjoy seeing my own work in print and I can read my own piece for several times and still enjoy it. I recognize good writing after reading the first few sentences. Patience is required to produce a quality piece of writing. Whenever possible I ask others to read through my work. I value their feedback and suggestions. Of course, you must have potential to write. Yes, you can do it if only you believe in yourself and you make writing fun. Nonetheless, to write well you ought to be an avid reader, you must read works of others and see how they do it. This is the reason you have to enjoy reading this book because you have passion for writing non-fiction.

This book may appeal to people who believe in the betterment of the human condition, freedom of the press, a better Africa, respect for others, self-esteem, a world free of guns, human rights, politics, and many such pertinent issues. I tackle issues that would be relevant and of interest to all good intentioned people. In other words this book will challenge you to start empathizing with the hundreds of million of people who live in abject poverty, who know no peace, who experience discrimination and it will also help you challenge your civic leaders to be accountable and live according to the ethics of love. Please, have the pleasure as you go through *A Robust Think Tank for Africa.*

Francis C. Chishala, S.J

Prologue

The media exist in a public sphere where market-place ideas are exchanged, challenged and developed. When reporting crime stories, does one always have to focus on the perpetrator or should the focus be on the victim or survivor? I applauded the stance taken by Anderson Cooper, CNN anchor of 360, in mid 2014 when he decided not to focus on the perpetrators of the school shootings that were occurring in many parts of the United States. Cooper decided to focus his reportage on the survivors; that is friends and families of the victims. The reason for the decision was that the perpetrators tend to seek attention. The media by focusing on them are actually making them heroes and somehow encouraging potential shooters or misfits.

Two hundred girls were abducted by the Boko Haram in the first quarter of 2014 and people the world over joined the "Bring back our girls' campaign." The early action or lack of action thereof of the Nigerian government failing to act swiftly had been condemned. My brother Jesuit and my former rector and lecturer, at the time provincial of the Jesuits of East Africa, Rev. Fr. Orobator Agbonkhianmeghe, S.J in his letter to president Jonathan Goodluck, vehemently castigated the Nigerian leader's lack of leadership in time of crisis like the abduction of the girls and requested for his resignation.

The future of the African child is at stake when we have heartless individuals and terrorist groups, whom I don't want to mention, commit heinous crimes because they are against the education of the girl child. While also the future of the African boy child is still at stake too with savages abducting them and recruiting them as child soldiers in the wars of the D.R Congo and Central Africa Republic. The girl child falls victim and becomes the survivor of rape. As an African, this robs my peace because tomorrow it could be my niece, nephew, sister, brother or neighbour being abducted or raped.

In Africa the neighbour's concern becomes your concern too, unless you choose to behave like the pig, cow and chicken in a story of the mouse. The story is told that one day the mouse discovered a trap set in the house and he decided to broadcast the news to the neighbours in the compound. The mouse first met the pig and reported the discovery to the pig and the pig brushed off the news saying it was none of his business. The mouse then met the cow and the cow like the pig bushed off the news saying she did not care as this had nothing to do with her. The mouse disappointed went off and found the hen. The hen responded like the others and she went on with her business. The mouse was devastated. When night came there was a big bang heard in the compound and the animals were scared. They started questioning what that could have been. It was the trap in the house that had caught a big snake. Unfortunately, the lady of the house woke up to check in the hallway what had happened. Since she had not put on the lights she stumbled upon the snake and got bitten. She was taken to the hospital and while there she developed a bad fever. The doctor prescribed chicken soup for her and the only chicken in the homestead was slaughtered to make the soup. Two weeks later she still wasn't feeling well. She had lost her appetite and all she needed was beacon. The only pig in the homestead was slaughtered in order to have beacon for the lady. A week later she lost hope and died. The husband had to slaughter a cow to feed the mourners for the week-long funeral. The mouse was relieved now that the funeral was over and he was safe. However, he went on beating his chest saying, "if only they had listened to me we could be happy together now." This is a moral dilemma for all of us.

Chapter One
An Issue of Human Rights

As a young Jesuit teaching in Mukasa Minor Seminary, Choma from the year 2003 to 2005, apart from the classroom situation, I had met a lot of people in the neighbourhood, whose lives were in a deplorable state. I had seen a lot of needy people flock our community house for assistance. Our community had been somehow turned into a social welfare institution. This is a common phenomenon in many Catholic religious houses in Zambia. The needy know that when things are tough, there are good people in the Catholic Church who would offer assistance. It is at this instance I realized how people appreciate the help that the Church offers to society. The Church ran a lot of institutions meant to uplift the human condition such as schools, hospitals, orphanages and youth centers. When I hear the argument that the Church ought to stick to the pulpit and not be involved in politics, I begin to wonder why the church should not. I have never heard of people complaining that the Church should not be involved in social work or health service provision.

The Catholic Church's main concern is to preach a gospel that brings liberation to the whole person. Hence, the Church would be doing disservice to itself if it cared only for the spiritual aspect and ignored the rest. The Church has to preach the gospel of hope that liberates humanity from all its bondage. The Church would not dare to keep silent when the human condition is in great misery. The Church would always seek appropriate ways of communicating in its quest to restore humanity's dignity and worthiness. Following these fundamental values, the Church seeks to promote human rights.

Human rights are individual's entitlements given to all in society. To speak of human rights we are talking of human dignity. It is evident that the creator in the order of creation inscribed these rights. States make concessions and declarations. These institutions express no more than what God Himself inscribed in the order of what he had created.

It is recognized that vulnerable groups in society such as children, women and the disabled need special covenants about their rights. These people need special rights because they are sometimes innocent, vulnerable and dependent.

Muna is one of the small boys who frequented our premises everyday at Mukasa Minor Seminary in Choma, Zambia. The boy was about 14 years of age. He came from a nearby compound called Chandamali. His regalia were dirty, greasy and smelly. The boy looked dark not because it was his natural complexion, no! It was a reflection of poverty. His clothes were dirty, greasy and smelly not because the mother was too lazy to wash them; no, the family could not simply manage to buy a packed of detergent.

His parents were poor and had no means of managing to feed and send Muna and his siblings to school.

The reason why Muna hung around Mukasa was that Mukasa was a place where he could find breakfast, lunch and supper, sometimes even a pair of shoes or clothing from the fathers' community. What actually Muna did with his friends whenever he was around Mukasa, was to wait for the pupils finish eating. Then he would collect the remains and sit to feast. At first, I thought he was collecting the food for the pigs, no! That was his meal.

This touched me. I knew that most of the minor seminarians were often touched, too, when they observed entrenched poverty before them. I would often see a minor seminarian give out part of his ration to Muna and the friends. At first, I had thought of chasing away Muna and his friends simply because I thought it was unhygienic to have them around the boarding school. I thought they would bring disease in the school. Later I realized I was scared to face the realities of poverty that Muna and his friends were representing day after day.

I decided to question the boy and find out why he was not in school. His answer was; 'I have no money to pay.' Was it not that primary education in Zambia was supposed to be free? Why then was it that Muna couldn't manage to be in school. Somebody in my religious community had actually paid for Muna to start school at a community school in Chandamali. I learnt why even after someone had paid for him and bought him books, still Muna was not in school. I was disarmed when he told me that he could not endure being in school on an empty stomach. The poor boy was hungry.

Did Muna deserve to be born of poor parents? No! The boy had no future, no hope. I would try to imagine what his life would be like in five or ten years' time. Would he always depend on charity? No, Muna deserved justice.

The story of Muna is not strange to any of us. We have all witnessed and encountered people living in abject poverty. We see boys and girls roaming our streets everyday with no sign of a better future. We have read features in the print media. We have watched documentaries about vulnerable people. I would imagine that we are always disturbed. We have seen children of the rich and looked at them assured of a bright future. Why the difference in the social and economic makeup of society?

Just observe when the grade nine results are announced each year. We often hear the statistics of pupils who had made the full certificate. It is not all of them who would be absorbed in the system to further their education. Actually, only a limited number would. For the rest, there are no places for them in the public schools. You would hear the minister of education announce, with a smiling face, that there are no places and government has no money. I recall at one time in Zambia the then minister of education tried to argue that education was not a right because it was not enshrined in the country's constitution.

I can go on giving a number of stories like that of Muna and friends but the point is; why do all of us not share the economic cake equally? This gives us the cause to promote human rights. This is simply fighting injustice in our midst through non-violence. Human rights should be protected by the rule of law.

The situation of Muna and many others, whose rights are ignored, is indeed redeemable only when those controlling the wheels of our nations' economy and the gears of public affairs create an atmosphere of equity. Yes, an atmosphere of equity where Muna as well as the children of 'kings' would all be given opportunities to education, health, food and shelter.

One of the American presidents Dwight D. Eisenhower once said:

> Every gun that is made, every warship launched, every rocket fired signifies in the final sense, a theft from those who hunger and are not fed, those who are cold and are not clothed. This world in arms is not spending money alone. It is spending the sweat of its labourers, the genius of its scientists, the hopes of its children. This is not a way of life at all in any true sense. Under the clouds of war, it is humanity hanging on a cross of iron (From a speech before the American Society of Newspaper Editors, April 16, 1953).

Reflection questions:

1. Do you think every country has an obligation to provide free education to its people or do you think people should provide for their own education?
2. If education is a human right, what is the implication of this for governments?
3. Do you know of stories like Muna's in your community?
4. Share a story of what you have seen in your neighbourhood?

Chapter Two
Unpalatable Utterances

It is pathetic to fathom some of the public utterances made by the political leaders in our beautiful land, Zambia. One wonders whether the leaders even listen to themselves when they speak. Occasionally, when one rebuts or gives them back their own words, the political leaders cry fowl by claiming that they are being quoted out of context. What do we hear? 'Education is not a right,' 'who is the government? I am the government,' 'NGO's entering and operating in a constituency without prior permission of the area M.P must be arrested,' 'the good harvest was due to good rains and not good policies.' Indeed, politics has become a talking shop where even the soft-spoken leaders make not only awful statements but also unimaginable statements.

Great leaders are often remembered by their philosophy gauged by what they said. Most often what they said would be rhetorical and perhaps unpopular yet they would hold on to a fact that society find difficult to come to terms with. Martin Luther king Jr. championed reconciliation through non-voilent resistance just like Mahatma Gandhi. Nelson Mandela also championed reconciliation through forgiveness. These charismatic leaders seized the opportunity to preach peace even when their followers expected a more aggressive approach in fighting the supposed enemy. Their own strength and glory was in their moving forward to embrace those who tortured them, those who killed their relations and friends, those who refused to respect their humanness and those who stood to extinguish their hope. These great leaders were extraordinary men in determinism and purpose.

In our beautiful land the political leaders make statements, I suspect, with an intention to be popular and not meaning what they say. This could be explained by the fact that the politicians refuse to take responsibility for what they had earlier said. When one utters what is unexpected from a rational leader it is obvious that the listeners would be perplexed and remain dumbfounded and much more ponder on the 'unsaid' that had been said and so as the listener ruminates on the 'unsaid' the picture and name of the 'parroting' leader hangs on. Each time he/she appears people would recognize him/her as that one who said this and that. Moreover, there are many ways of becoming known, either good or bad ways. One could be known by being talented, holding position of responsibility or in a negative sense being a drunk and misbehaving in the public.

Some politicians because of lack of ideas tend to use public forums to attack institutions that stand for justice and truth. As citizens of our beautiful country we have rights to many things. We should not be passive citizens when it comes to the political affairs of our land. We are the ones who elect the political leaders with the hope that they would deliver the services that will lead our beautiful land to prosperity and development. The mandate that we bestow on the political leaders is that they would listen to the masses and be able to translate the people's ideals into programs and policies that would be of benefit to our land. It is unacceptable for political leaders to attack and label charitable organizations, NGO's, religious institutions and many such that provide check and balances as opponents. These organizations are supposed to be regarded as partners in development. Politicians come and go but these bodies are always available in supporting the efforts of government. To ever think that NGO's and religious institutions provide services to the marginalized and poor for political ends is an insult to these well meaning. These institutions have done much in this country and it is a known fact that government could not manage to do it alone.

The only way the political leaders would be confrontational with NGOs and Religious bodies is when they feel threatened, incapacitated and ashamed for not meeting the aspirations of the people.

My advice to the political leaders is that they should strive to tell the truth and much more pray before they open their mouths in public and not to open their mouths before they 'prey' on the masses.

Every citizen and institution has a moral and social responsibility to its immediate environment. It is not for the politicians to grant us permission to do what is noble for our country and people. It is for us as good citizens to demand and ask politicians to fulfill their promises. Our electing them was not to make them bosses or despot over us but servants of the people. If they (politicians) cannot beat the many institutions that are providing great service to the nation then they should emulate these institutions and not embarrass themselves by unpopular and awful utterances.

Questions for reflection:

1. Have you ever thought why sometimes politicians don't tell the truth or keep their promises?
2. How do you make politicians accountable to the voters by fulfilling their campaign promises?
3. How do you encourage servant-leadership in your local civic leaders?

Chapter Three
Communication in the workplace

Purpose of communication in an organization.

Communication has a greater role to play in an organization for effectiveness and efficiency. Effective communication is multi-dimensional and it serves different purposes depending on which direction or level it is operating on. This discourse looks at the dynamics of effective communication at three levels articulating its purpose and impact on the organization as a whole.

In an organization we can speak of communication at three distinct levels; namely top-down communication, upward communication, and horizontal communication.

Top – down communication:

This is communication that goes on from management to the employees. Five of its functions are the following:

i) To convey information or give directives in order to influence behavior that leads to achieving organizational goals. Managers avoid leaving employees with gaps in information. The managers give information and directives for the work as early as possible before the employees decide to embark on the task assigned. When plans change or there is a crisis, effective managers exercise emotional intelligence when communicating in order to avoid being alarmists. Effective managers communicate crises with a deep concern and awareness on how this would impact the employees.

ii) To ensure understanding – this involves managers giving to as well as receiving feedback from the employees. The manager communicates in such a way that employees feel confortable to ask for clarification when instruction are not clear. In return employees give feedback in an appropriate manner.

iii) To get action – to motivate others or getting things done through people and this requires skill and tact. The manager by communicating the nature of the task and the role of the employee in carrying it out, motivates the employees to welcome the assignment and to get to action as though the employee were doing what she/he likes most.

iv) To persuade – making others buy into the goals and vision of the organization and thereby taking responsibility for their collective participation. Effective managers make sure they communicate their vision and also the core-shared values of the organization clearly. They make the employees understand what the task is and what is expected of them and how this is also important to them. Effective managers make the employees feel part of a team and that they are there to add value and contribute to the achievement of the organization's objectives and goals by successfully completing organizational tasks assigned them successfully.

v) To build relationship – effective managers do not only give instructions and directives to the employees but sometimes they also engage in talk that indicate concern and interest in the employees, each of them as a person. Effective managers do this by simple things that matter like a greeting, a birthday wish or a joke. They create a rapport and make the employee open up and feel accepted and valued not only as a worker but also as an individual.

Upward communication:
Employees communicating with management.

This type of communication addresses three important purposes:

i) It offers suggestions and input - how an employee responds to the instruction, directives or information. When the task is well communicated and the employee understands the values and goals of the organization, it is very easy for him/her to appropriate the core-shared values by feeling part of the team. This, as it were, makes the employee open up and share his/her ideas about the task and ask appropriate questions to guide him/her carry out the task with diligence and skill knowing that his/her input matters.

ii) It seeks clarification to avoid rumors and misunderstanding – when employees feel they belong they ask the right questions at the right time to the right person and they by all means avoid grapevine or rumours. Once there is a good rapport everyone in the workplace feels a sense of responsibility and determinism.

iii) It aims at seeking understanding the vision and goals of the organization – the employee will have a sense of self-determinism because he/she has grasped the manager's vision and the goals of the establishment. By accepting the core-shared values the employee is able to communicate this through the way he/she responds to instructions and directives either through verbally or non- verbally cues. For instance, responding positively by putting in the best or negatively by social loathing.

Horizontal (peer to peer) communication:
Three aims of horizontal communication are:

i) To share ideas and suggestions in relation to the common task being pursued by workmates. Many a time employees are called to work as a team therefore the need to communicate among themselves. As co-operation and corroboration is required, employees communicate ideas and suggestions concerning the common task that they have. In their communication they validate each other and also correct each other when mistakes occur.

ii) To ask for clarification or support in executing the task – each employee is aware of the task or the role she/he is supposed to play in the group and also take particular interest in what others are doing. This awareness facilitates proper exchange of ideas and suggestions among core workers.

iii) Building relationships and trust among co-workers – bonding among employees is very important and this is achieved through talking to each other in an open manner about the task and about other personal issues. Talking to each other about many things opens up relationships and creates an environment where corroboration is valued against competition, dialogue is valued against debate, and correction and confrontation is taken positively and seen as an aid to creating proper understanding in the present and the future.

Dangers of lack of effective communication:

i) Lack of a sense of a shared vision and purpose:
When management communicates effectively they ensure smooth transfer of the organization's goals and the vision of the management to employees. Lack of proper communication from management to employees affects the performance of employees. Without this communication the employees will have no sense of what the organization stands for and what they have to achieve collectively through their input.

ii) Lack of understanding or taking on the values of the organization – team spirit becomes low. The management by constantly sharing information with the employees they somehow create a picture of what values the organization hold. Failure by management to communicate well translates into the employees' misunderstanding of the organizational values and thereby thwarting creativity and innovativeness in the employees.

iii) Selfishness and unhealthy competition – When management fails to communicate instructions and information to the employees this leads to employees seeking their own fulfillment at the expense of the organization and thereby causing unhealthy competition and selfishness among themselves. This is the same when employees fail to communicate among themselves. The result is selfishness, which diverts attention from reaching organizational goals to workers fighting for recognition and favouratism.

iv) When management communicates well with employees they expect to receive feedback. Lack of feedback can injure the smooth functioning of the organization as a whole.

Recommendations for effective communication to managers and employees:

Management should ensure that it communicates effectively to the employees and that it understands the different personality types of their employees. Instructions and information should be given to employees ahead of time. The employees should have an understanding of what the management expects of them in the workplace. A good rapport between management and the employees ensures effectiveness and efficiency in the operations and functioning of the organization. Good communication in the workplace by all stakeholders brings motivation especially among the employees and enhances high performance. Communication in the organization takes on many facets, as it can be verbal and non-verbal. Therefore it is incumbent upon management to understand how to use and read both verbal and non-verbal cues when dealing with employees for the betterment of the organizations.

Management should be trained in communication skills for the workplace because communication is the heart of organizations. Communication affects organizational behavior among employees and management and thereby influences its overall out-put. Face to face communication should be valued in order to build relationships. But also written communication should follow especially on issues of contracts, promotions and policies.

Questions for reflection:

1. Can you pick anyone with positional power that inspires you?
2. What makes the individual of your choice stand out more than others?
3. What makes a good leader and a good manager?
4. Do you think managers or leaders of today communicate well?
5. What is the definition of good communication in the workplace for you?

Chapter Four
Africa's Economic Emancipation

The question of Africa moving out of its poverty and coming to realize its wealth of numerous natural and human resources has floundered due to its nihilism and pessimism. These negative emotional and mental attitudes grow out of a mistrust in African governments that they have been incapable of delivering what they have promised. The common trend in African governments has been a lack of political will in transforming Africa's economy from international donor dependency to a locally driven and generated economy.

There are many vices that have gripped most African political leaders to such a point that they are incapacitated in distributing the nation riches equally with the ordinary citizens. Greed, corruption, nepotism and arrogance have led some African leaders to forget to plan and manage their economy and states. As a result of poor planning, some African leaders have willingly danced to the tune of the international donor community and unwisely permitted both rich conglomerates and individuals with wealth to use the world's tax havens and banking systems to siphon sums of money out of Africa. Africa having attained political emancipation in the last sixty years the expectations were that with this political emancipation economic autonomy would follow, a hope arched in Kwame Nkrumah's philosophy "seek ye first the political freedom and the other freedoms would be added unto you". What has gone wrong in Africa's journey towards a total economic emancipation? It is very important to ponder this question so as to gain insight into the conceptualization and devising appropriate measures of charting a new path to Africa's economic liberation. Has political liberation failed Africa? Is democracy failing Africa? If not, then why is it that Africa still needs international donor aid, conditionality and neocolonialism?

Given the good news of the Jubilee Debt Cancellation and Make Poverty History campaign having succeeded in the past decade and more aid flowing, what is next in Africa's war of alleviating poverty as per millennium goals? The prophets of doom for Africa argue that even with debt cancellation and receiving aid from abroad, Africa will still remain impoverished. They have claimed that continuous assistance to Africa, though well intentioned, will never solve Africa's problems. They base their pessimism on the presumption that most of the aid given to Africa does not reach the intended people. Rather it ends up in the bureaucratic structures that are ill-functional and inefficient. Though most patriotic Africans' would not buy into this pessimism, to some extent it has a point that needs to be considered in order to raise the hope of a total economically liberated Africa.

Africa needs a vibrant civil service with a capacity to deliver. The civil service in Africa lacks the capacity to deliver the national resource and the international donor aid down to the very peasant in society. The civil service is poorly organized primarily because it is intertwined in nepotism at the expense of professionalism. This stultifies the civil service because you would not expect relatives of government officials heading a civil service to perform, though they could be exceptions if such are qualified. African statesmen, from Nkwame Khruma, to Thabo Mbeki, to Robert Mugabe, to Paul Kagame, to Jacob Zuma and the NEPAD crew, have blown the horn for Africa taking responsibility of its own destiny. Without commitment to this challenge, even with a debt free and elimination of corruption, Africa would still fail to distribute its resources to the poor person. Botswana is isolated as a success story in having the capacity to distribute the benefits of its mineral resources to the very poor person in the rural areas. However, it could be asserted that the way forward for Africa calls for political leaders having a political will in the process of developing its own political muscle. In sum, Africa must begin looking to itself in redressing and addressing its economic and developmental nightmares.

Some observers in the West have thought of another intervention. They suggest recolonizing Africa with a project of demarcating Africa's geographical and political boarders into states that have a reason to ethnically exist together. While this is an expression of independent and free thought, the idea is a joke, however it merits some serious thought on the future of Africa as it strikes a point that would make African leaders and intellectuals to start thinking. For instance, Africa needs a revolution in political leadership in order for its future to brighten. For instance, Liberia's President, Johnson Sirleaf (just thinking aloud) as an experienced economist, perhaps it is a pointer to a millennium package indicating new leadership style capable of influencing and effecting change.

The early 1990's witnessed the shift of African governments from one-party state to multi-party politics. This shifting to multi-party politics had introduced a new, three-tier democratic system that brought together politicians or governments, economic communities (investors) and civil society on the same table in the process of defining national development and interest, the Zambian and South African situation are success stories. The partnership of government, civil society and the economic community is perhaps a good starting point in Africa's move towards taking full responsibility in managing its own political and economic affairs. The civil society, as it were, provides for the monitoring and enhancement of good governance. It is the responsibility of governments in Africa to engineer political and economical change; however, the civil society plays a major role especially in reaching the grassroots. What is required is for a commitment by government's in creating an enabling environment that would favour and promote local investments. The government's role is to create policies that encourage the civil society partner with the economic community in empowering the masses. Through this partnership, the riches and national resources would be able to reach the common person at the bottom of society.

The question to be asked today is whether Africa, after the ushering in of democracy has continued to make progressive steps in the distribution of resources to all. Is there a sign that Africa would achieve economic liberation? With the three-tier partnership the future of Africa is bright. Everywhere in Africa, countries have started addressing issues of corruption, though not with a desired speed. The consolation for Africa's success comes when history indicates that even the developed world took years to reach where they are at now. Africa has all the able resources, both natural and human, to mitigate its economic difficulties. What is required is the change of attitude and an assumption of a political aggressivity that would make the civil service to function with vibrancy. The international community either civil or religious has opted to talk of Africa as a frontier in the sense that Africa is not only a place the world should adopt for rescue missions but a frontier in which there is potential to tap in through support and encouragement.

Questions for reflection:

1. Do you believe that the problem lies with leadership in Africa or simply it is cultural?
2. What is your understanding of Africa as a frontier?
3. What model of leadership in the African traditional society reflects the spirit of commitment and stewardship? Do you believe that the problem of Africa today was as a result of the scramble for Africa in the early 1880's?

Chapter Five
Respect the differences

When we think of atrocities that have been associated with history, we realize that humanity had fallen to subhuman standards when dialogue had ceased to exist. The many challenges that face humanity are well addressed when people begin to dialogue. Adolf Hilter had great persuasive power that he managed to convince his listeners with anti-semantic views and the rest is history. History has been replicated with different forms and shapes of philosophies of resistance. Martin Luther King, Malcolm X and Marvin Gaye championed the civil rights movement at a time that humanity used race to discriminate one race by another, denying others their humanness. Just like the civil rights movement championed equality of all people regardless of colour, Mandela and many South Africans, both black and white spoke against apartheid. In South Africa a fundamentalist approach to the Christian text was used to argue for the superiority of one race over the other just like the same text was used to argue for the slave trade. Fundamentalism through selective reading used the text to perpetrate inhuman behaviors of discrimination. Thus it missed the whole principle of the golden rule to love the other in the same way one loves the self, and to do to the other what one would want to be done to him or her.

Apparently, Nelson Mandela and Almicar Cabral both taught that not only were they fighting white oppression but that it would be sorry to see another black person oppressing the other. Slavery and racism might have been erased in society in as far as we might want to believe. But new forms of oppression and discrimination do exist and humanity is still using the same canons of selective reading of scripture. The philosophy of resistance exists and is championed by those who are discriminated because of their social status and denied opportunities due to poverty. It is championed by those who are discriminated against because of their gender or ethnicity. It is championed by those who are judged, denied a voice and sometimes killed because of their sexual orientation. Humanity should learn to interpret those religious texts that speak about a universal spirit of love, and not emphasizing only the text that fits ones' agenda. For instance, some religious texts speak vehemently against fornicators and adulterers as not fit for the kingdom. Yet while people are very careful not to condemn them they may take seriously a passage that condemns same sex encounters. We all know stories of lesbians and gay people who have been brutally murdered because of their sexual orientation. Ugandan and Zimbabwean presidents have been adamant about allowing gay and lesbian rights. They have even made outrageous sentiments that demean and deny personhood and humanness to those who have dared to come in the open and declare their sexual orientation. Museveni says it is scientifically proven that homosexuality is a learned tendency and not a biological trait. The European Union (EU) and the Obama administration have been very clear whether in Russia or Uganda or Zimbabwe that no one should be denied their humanness and personhood because of sexual orientation.

Some sections of society in Africa argue wrongly that homosexuality is un-African and that it is foreign and a sickness. Homosexuality is a universal reality that Africans should stop to deny. Talk of the Bunganda kingdom in the 18th century, the king was gay and did not learn it from the foreigners or the westerners. The universal ethics of love calls humanity to treat differences and preferences with due respect. Certain cultures in Africa would kill people with albinism because of strange beliefs or children who were left handed would be forced to use the right hand failing to realize that the other is different yet fully human. It is high time that Africa should begin to dialogue and realize that denying someone his or her rights because of sexual orientation is a terrible sin against humanity like slave trade and apartheid are.

The new battle in the world is to speak against discrimination of any form and to call for mutual love, respect and appreciation of diversity and differences. South Africa and some western countries have championed universal human rights that do not discriminate against gender, race, religious affiliation, sexual orientation and status in life. We are all first human beings and equal before the law. We have no right to think badly of someone else because he or she is different from us. Humanity should begin to think that those who are different from us in whatever way have the same rights and should enjoy the same rights like us all. The Ugandan and South African experience of one loosing life because of sexual orientation is an experience that should not have happened and should not be let to happen again. Our African leaders should call for dialogue over such issues and educate the masses to appreciate differences and otherness because lack of dialogue only perpetrates oppression and discrimination of the worse kind. Humanity should learn to listen because it is our sons and daughters that we are tormenting by denying them their voices and freedom of expression and association, which are fundamental human rights.

Emeritus archbishop of Cape Town and social activities Desmond Tutu has been very consistent and categorical in speaking against discrimination of any form because he stands for justice and respect of human values. The likes of Mandela and Tutu were called names for speaking against black oppression by whites. Tutu stood his ground and remained true to his calling to speak against class oppression even in the black government. Today Tutu, like Mandela, continues to raise his voice against class, social, gender and sexual discrimination. People should desist from using religious texts to champion their narrow agenda. Instead they ought to glow with a love that recognizes humanity and personhood in the other and thereby promote mutual existence and appreciation. Those who might be different from you do not simply need your tolerance, they need your respect; not only your understanding also your acceptance. Denying them a listening ear only reduces you to barbaric ways of acting. Pope Francis' words, "Who am I to judge?" Ought to move us to a new approach to life that respects and values coexistence, the beauty and richness of diversity. Our leaders in Zambia, Malawi, South Africa, Zimbabwe and elsewhere in Africa should begin the dialogue to build understanding and desists from appealing to a false and imagined African canon to deny a universal reality that is enshrined in the universal human rights declaration; the respect and non-discrimination of anyone due to differences in race, gender, religious, political, economical, sexual orientation and other human values.

Questions for reflection:

1. What is the value of accepting and respecting differences among peoples?
2. Do you think this approach leads to relativism and wearing out of fundamental values in society?

3. Do you find it difficulty to accept people who have values different from yours?
4. How would you promote understanding and respect of difference in today's society?

Chapter Six
The Culture of Silence

A 'culture of silence' is a detriment to the holistic evolution of any society's ethics. This 'culture of silence' that is so prominent in our society is as a result of certain cultural norms that value age and position at the expense of truth, accountability and transparency. Only a few members of our society dare challenge the cultural 'status quo' that has little to offer to the well being of society. I am referring to people who are able to pick-out bad elements of culture and speak against them without fear.

Take for instance Maiwa, a sixteen year old, young girl living in rural Chama, who is sexually abused by her father, the sole breadwinner in the family. Who does Maiwa report to? Does she tell her mother, who also fears divorce? Does she report to the local police, who have a record of abusing female detainees? Does she confide in her teachers or pastors or priests, some of who are also culprits in abusing those under their responsibility? Most often, due to shame and lack of trust to those around her, Maiwa may decide to keep silent over the issue for fear that when she reports to her mother she will not be understood or she will be silenced for fear of bringing the household's name into disrepute.

The culture of silence grows from such domestic situations to the other strata of society such as the school, the church, the workplace and nation. People are afraid to speak out against any social injustices prevailing in their milieu for fear of being victimized or harassed. At work people decide to keep quiet over issues of mismanagement, corruption or abuse for fear of being victimized through the lose of employment. At other levels like politics, people might decide to be silent perhaps because they are beneficiaries of corruption or perhaps because they feel connected with the abuser and they do not want to fall out of favour. Reasons of people keeping quiet over issues of concern are innumerable.

Speaking out is important to the development, growth and sustainability of society. We should differentiate the 'culture of silence' from introverts versus extroverts. What is meant by speaking-out is different from making noise or waffling, so common among politicians and fake preachers. Positive criticism is what speaking-out entails. Most often, despots and those adults who hide behind culture are scared of positive criticism. They would claim that they want positive criticism and when it comes their way they cry foul because this injures their fake 'crocodile' skin that is nothing but a pig's intestine.

Most often when people meet in public places such as the market place, the shopping center, the pub and many such places, they discuss varied topics depending on their interests. Some people would go crazy talking about soccer or other sports; others would talk about issues of bread and butter; some would talk about their work, children, school and many other such topics. It is so interesting to notice ordinary people engage in what may seem as small talk, for instance talking football, food, sex, politics and gossiping about others. The latter interests me, though I regard gossiping as a vent for what has to be spoken out but is being spoken to the wrong people at a wrong time and in fear that those spoken about might hear.

Some years ago I was in a minibus along the Great East Road, Lusaka commuting from Marshlands to Showgrounds, when I overheard the driver gossip about a friend who had fallen from the grace of prosperity to the status of a destitute. The story goes that the fellow was brought up by a rich father, a farmer, who had provided everything from education to finding a job for the fellow. When the father died the son inherited all the wealth. Surprisingly, the fellow turned to a high and wayward life of drinking and womanizing. After a few years, the fellow sold the farm, the car and the minibus he had bought from his father's pension. Then the fellow began selling household goods. It was clear that the next step the fellow was going to sell the house. Though I thought this was gossiping, I later realized that this story tells much about what goes on in society. People like to gossip, perhaps for the benefits of those listening. I, in particular, learned from this gossip and started reflecting on my own life. Dear readers I bet you, too, have something to learn from the gossiping that goes around. However, speaking-out in defense of justice as well as advising friends are the best solution. It is no good to wait until things are bad that is when you open your mouth.

Those few people who challenge the cultural 'status quo' never give up even when they feel intimidated. It is better to face a friend and tell him/her what you feel than telling others about him/her. When despots react it is time to speak even more forcefully because you will realize that it is the truth. No wonder it hurts those who hear it. The media, both press and electronic, have become public spheres where social, political, economical, gender and other such discourses are carried out. The media manage to offer citizens a picture of what is at play in society. There are sections of society that 'trust' or believe in the media and regard them as a source of information. There are also others who do not believe at all anything they read in the press or watch on television. And there are segments of society that approach the media with a critical mind, people who critically analyze what they read, watch or listen, people with the ability to know what they ought to take and what they ought to discard. At the end of it all, the media are the best 'public space' for social, economic, political and other discourses.

In the first and second republic in Zambia we had party cadres who would harass anyone who opposed the government of the day. We had party women escorting the head of state and dancing at the airport. Some of these women were party cadres and others were marketeers, who had no option but dance for the 'leader.' It is sad today to see that party cadres fail to distinguish state or national functions with party functions. The state president is for both those who elected him/her and those citizens of the state who did not elect him/her. When the state president is criticized by patriotic citizens it is not up to party cadres to issue threats, such occurrences only happen in autocratic states and are alien to democratic states.

In a 'baby' democracy there is a likelihood of autocratic tendencies to resurface. Take for instance a president elected by a minority might not have the support of the entire electorate, say the seventy-so percent that did not vote for him/her. In order for this leader to protect his endangered ego he/she aught to put up a despotic muscle to threaten even those who offer positive criticism, rest they expose the leader's weaker point.

A patriotic citizen would criticize when criticism is due and offer credit when credit is due. I believe most people in our country will learn to vote for the person who can deliver and is accountable to the electorate, a person who is wise and listens to the wishes of the people. That is why we need a president with a fifty plus one vote who would be a true representative of the majority.

The danger of a minority president is that both he/she and the minority (party cadres) feel threatened by positive criticism and act less like despots.

At the stage of democracy in our country, what we need is to register as voters in numbers and make sure, during election time, we cut the 'culture of silence' by speaking out through the ballot, where no one intimidates or harasses others.

Questions for reflection:

1. Why do people in certain cultures fear to challenge their leaders or speak the truth to their leaders?
2. What issues in your society do you think people shun away and talk about behind the back of the person concerned?

Chapter Seven
The Press in a Democratic Africa

In any democratic dispensation elections' time is the pinnacle of democracy. It is during this period that the test for democracy becomes apparent. However, elections could not be classified as the only measure of democracy. There are other serious tenets of democracy like good governance, upholding of the rule of law, promotion of human rights, a free press and separation of powers in the three organs of the state among many other things. In the West the media can be said to wield a lot of power due to the fact that people rely on the media for information about many things; for instance, the way government is run. This aspect of the media somehow cannot be true if we were to consider most parts of Africa. In Africa most media outlets; like newspapers, are not easily accessible to the majority of the population that live in remote areas and under abject poverty. The implication of this is that not so many Africans can manage to buy a copy of a newspaper everyday for 365 days. Worse still, the illiteracy levels in Africa are so high. Very few newspapers are published in African or in indigenous languages, hence leaving many Africans with an information blackout. Broadcasting through radio is one way through which the African media have been able to reach the majority of the rural folks because with radio the issue of illiteracy does not count. although the media does not wield much power in Africa, they at least play a major role in the democratic process of a country. However, newspaper publications unlike radio broadcast can be kept and shared even by the poor for a longer period. For a rural folk a week old newspaper is not old news at all if one were accessing it for the first time.

In most parts of Africa the press is unregulated and it is divided between state-owned and independent or privately owned newspapers. It has always been the case that the state owned newspapers trails the government line by acting as its propaganda tool. On the other hand the independent press has added a new angle in reporting African politics. The independent press in Africa has been known to champion causes of a free press and has unearthed stories of corruption in public office. However, the independent press has been accused of sensationalising political issues in its reportage and often has faced unruly party cadres' harassment and government's wrath of every kind; including imprisonment of people of the press.

With the beginning of multi-party politics and liberal democracy in Africa, after the collapse of the Berlin wall, much has been expected of the media especially in sustaining and fostering the tenets of democracy. Having lived with the government controlled press in the past, the African populace expects the privately controlled press to act as an alternative voice. Just as the state-controlled press is biased towards the ruling party and champions the ideals of the government in power, the privately owned press is also constrained by market forces to endorse according to vested interests, certain positions that might seem to be biased against the government's position on a number of issues. However, the living side by side of the government-controlled press with the independent press contributes to the fostering and sustenance of democracy. Some of the tenets of democracy include a free press and free and fair elections. In the discourse of press and democracy one of the most important virtues is that people or the public have access to information; right information for that matter, to enable them to exercise their democratic rights. For instance, during political elections, people are free to elect a leader of their choice. It is in this respect that the media; and the press in particular, are seen to play a significant role in democracy. It is in reporting politics that a disparaging contrast between government controlled press and privately controlled press can be noticed. One particular moment this can be noticed is during political campaign and elections.

The African press has realised that the African readership takes particular interest in the political life of their nations. It is political news, reports and stories that usually take the headlines of the majority of the African newspapers. However, it is little known whether the press influences the African populace on whom to vote for during parliamentary and presidential elections.

There has been a tendency by politicians in Africa to use the press in order to gain political mileage. However, when the press initiates stories that implicate a particular politician then you hear calls of respect for privacy. The democratic dispensation calls for a free media and unregulated press. The

African situation presents us with a two-tier approach to the press; that is state-controlled and independent or private-controlled. What role is the press in Africa expected to play in this epoch? Are there different roles for private-controlled press and for the state-controlled press? Or does the press have a common role either as private-controlled or state-controlled?

It is argued that a free press and mostly an independent press can be more effective than an opposition party in bringing about change in an oppressive regime. Much more in a democracy the press can be effective also in unearthing corruption and bad governance. A free press is a pillar of democracy because it provides check and balances for the ruling elite and government. The press has often been referred to as the fourth estate. As the fourth estate the press has a watchdog role to play in society. In short, the press should act as the conscience of society. Therefore, the role of the press is not only to report about what the government is doing but also to bring out issues of public interest that politicians sometimes ignore. It can also monitor and follow up politicians to see if they are living up to their promises. It is not a bad thing to have an opposition press in a situation where the state also owns a number of newspapers. If state-owned newspapers are going to tell us about the government and its programmes, then an independent press is a relief to save us from propaganda. The independent press therefore would be needed to offer an alternative voice. Usually a free press reinforces democratic ideals. A state-owned press has a public mandate to serve the public interest and the national interest. National interest and public interest are not a prerogative for those who wield political power or financial power but for the general populace. Knowing that the private-press is sometimes moved by market interest this does not stop it from serving public interest and national interest. It is at this point that the issue of media ethics and professional integrity become imperative. The press has a role of agenda setting on issues such as the economy, health, education, employment and constitution. The list can go on. The media and the press in particular have to reclaim their credibility through critical and in-depth analysis of issues. Election time is a time of decision-making and it is only with a free press that people can be able to do that effectively and efficiently.

What has been lacking in the African press is good, adept and in-depth analysis of issues. These qualities demands that the press do thorough research on an issue and present it professionally rather than angling it to fit the press's interests. Good, adept and in-depth analysis presents facts as they are and leaves the reader with the duty to draw his/her own conclusions. For instance, during election campaign, the press could do good research on the political parties contesting focusing on the party manifesto and the programs the party is pushing. Dwelling too much on personalities defeats the ideal of professionalism. It would rather be necessary to highlight what the candidates have to offer and to discuss their credentials. What has been the case in most African press is the focus on petty personality issues that are counter-productive to the exercise of true democracy. The African press ought to be able to discern what is the right information for the readership at each particular time. Sometimes when it comes to serving national interest and upholding peace it is very important for the press to be vigilant on what information they disseminate. A free press does not imply a lack of responsibility on the side of the press. What is needed in today's democratic Africa is a press that is responsible in making our leaders accountable to the electorate of their actions. However, a courageous press is one that is capable of taking risks in the quest of promoting the tenets of democracy.

Questions for reflection:

1. Do you think the media wield much power in society today?
2. Why should people not believe what they read in the media sometimes?
3. Are the media in Africa serving their function and role? What is this function and role?

Chapter Eight

The 'Za-yellow' Phenomenon

I recall some years ago standing at the old Lusaka CR bus terminus behind the Bank of Zambia trying to get a ticket for a coach for Kitwe, when a white man disembarks from a bus that had just arrived. A minute later his African female partner also disembarks. At first glance my friend and I, and of course the other people around, thought our dear lady is white. She was light in complexion like orange juice and had what seemed like blonde hair. Her mannerism of walking was closely observed. Her waist swings evenly oscillated like a pendulum.

The lady had drawn much attention to herself. I thought perhaps people are excited for having seen a white lady, a common phenomenon in rural areas but not in Lusaka. But this is Lusaka, what is the fuss all about? People started murmuring and giggling, and all eyes moved towards our lady. Whoosh! Our lady had put on a pair of jeans and a long sleeve pullover. Her arms were charcoal black. I turned towards my friend, who upon catching my glance exploded into laughter. "Is the lady from the States, England or China?" I asked. My friend laughed even louder. Often, I am fond of asking bleached skinned men and women if they are from a Western or Eastern country.

It is a common phenomenon among some ladies; and some men too, to bleach their skin. Most do it perfectly well by an injection and the whole body becomes bleached. The lady in question seems to have missed art-classes in her elementary school years to end up with such a poor aesthetic perception. By just applying Ambi or other cosmetics on her face and ignoring the rest of her body what was she thinking about? Did she really have a vision of what she really wanted to look like or did she just plunge herself into an expedition she had no clue about? Okot P'Bitek in *Song of Lawino* describes people who bleach their skin, in the character of Clementine, as fakes, people with a colour psychosis. In fact in Zambia such people are popularly referred to as "Za-yellow" and in the D.R.C, were the trend is so popular they are known as "Phenomenon Choco."

A common argument made is that such people are so much indoctrinated into believing that anything black is angry and anything light or white is beautiful. Also that ones own natural hair is not beautiful, only the hair stolen from white ladies is beautiful, that is if these white ladies were alive but at most it is the hair of dead people, cats, horses even dogs.

All of us apply some cosmetics on our bodies for one reason or the other. To leave the skin, hair, teeth and whatever unattended to would not do as any good as it would make our appearance apathetic to those we meet. It is important to look presentable. Somehow, our appearance and the way we take care of it strikes a point and adds on our self-esteem. Taking care of ones appearance involves much energy and requires great aesthetic appreciation and know-how.

There is a misconception that if you are lighter, people may tend to like you more than the darker types. I, for one, appreciate natural beauty, those who are naturally lighter and those who are naturally darker in complexion. What is important is to know how to manage and maintain your natural beauty. Changing the colour of ones skin is just going too far. It is really quite interesting to see that people want to look beautiful by applying all sorts of cosmetics but the end result is that most of them look miserable. I don't know if these people ever take trouble to check themselves in the mirror. Worse still these cosmetics, in old age, cause a lot of damage on the skin such as the 'come to stay' marks.

I have found out, through observation, that the phenomenon of bleaching ones skin is not so popular among the younger educated generation. It is more common with people with little education with an appearance complex or crisis.

I have no difficulty with people who dress in fashion. I get puzzled when people attack the younger generation on their style of dress. For the young, it is a way of expressing themselves, a way of struggling with identity crisis, and at most conforming to the dictates of globalization. This is a stage worth passing through. If the young were to be controlled and told what they have to wear and look like, things would turn upside down when they get older and become independent. Just consider some of your friends who were brought up by very strict parents, what has happened to them? Most of them are drunks and a nuisance to society.

To condemn the young that they do not dress appropriately is in someway projecting the difficulties one faces in accepting what one did not go through. In a nutshell, it is a refusal to accept change and to accept the fact that the new generation is moving faster in all spheres of life.

One would not expect the young to pass through exactly the same processes that characterized one's growth. In the past the young would always learn from the old. Today things are different. With the innovations of the information and communication technology (ICTs) the old are now learning from the young. How many parents know how to manipulate the gargets of technology in their homes? Mostly, it is the young who are called to assist. Talk of cell phones, mostly elders know only how to receive and send a call, as for computers only to process and print documents and nothing else.

Talking about the 'Za-Yellows' phenomenon, I realize that the trend became so pronounced in the early years of the third republic. I remember the second republican president once bragging about the benefits of the liberalized economy that our ladies are now looking beautiful because of using 'Interchem' (cosmetics). Just as everything has its positive and negative side, the 'globalised' cosmetics of the third republic have left us people with corrupt skins that have come to stay.

The task for the current leadership and the next is to see how Zambia could also become a contributor and equal player on the global market.

It is disheartening these days to hear high profile politicians engage in nothing but insults. It would be unfortunate and embarrassing for the generations of our Zambian leaders to be identified with nothing but insults and locking-up opponents and critics. Perhaps, these would be as a result of the 'politics of cosmetics,' the 'Za-Yellow' phenomenon, a lighter face with black arms.

Our politicians, especially those aspiring for presidency, should have a clear vision of why they want to ascend to that office and what they have to offer to the Zambian people. Otherwise, it would be sorry for them getting there and realizing that they do not have even a single clue of what it means to be head of state. Lack of vision would lead into a president lacking focus of the essentials and only to meddle in petty personality-directed issues of no relevance to the development and growth of our beloved Zambia. The only way to guarantee that Zambia rid itself from myopic and 'cosmetic' leadership is for the citizens to exercise their voting rights when the time to vote is due. It would actually be better if a few candidates, say three or four, were to contest for presidency unlike a situation where ten or more contest. With the latter you might end up with a president imposed on you by the minority, a president awaken from sleep to contest against his/her desires, and the end result would be a disastrous leader who is scared of his/her own shadow.

Questions for reflection:

1. What is your take on skin bleaching and self-esteem?

Chapter Nine

Connected by a click

The new technological innovations have enhanced human communication and have also defied the odds in terms of human interaction. A new bond has been created among people separated by distance. A new language uniting people has been established through new media and social media. Kenneth Burke's theory of communication augurs well with the scenario created by new media and social media that presents a dichotomy between separateness and identification in human interaction.

Burke in his work, *A Rhetoric of Motives* (1969) distinguishes the traditional notion of rhetoric as focused on "persuasion" by the use of the term "identification." He notes that as human beings we experience alienation from the moment of birth though we are part of a family or community. We feel both the connectedness and the separation, hence the need to feel identified. For Burke, identification is paramount to communicating and it is a process of being human. As human beings we feel alienated from others because we believe in order and hierarchy. This separateness or alienation is multifaceted as it could be either biological or based on social class or position. Due to class separation we are caught up in the sin of "us" and "them" following the different placements in the hierarchy.

Further still, Burke sees human interactions, in our contemporary society, as complicated in some way. Human beings seek identification through communication to overcome the separateness. According to Burke the ambiguity or the tension that exists between being separated and being identified are so pronounced in our society today. He sees identification as compensatory to separation. He postulates that we build social cohesion through the use of language, which is a symbolic action. Human beings are actors and the use of language is one way of acting in the world. Hence,

Burke defines rhetoric as "the use of words by human agents to form attitudes or induce actions in other human agents." Burke's identification has three dimensions, namely (i) the process of naming something according to certain properties, (ii) the process of associating with and disassociating from others, and (iii) the end result of identifying.

In contemporary communication we find also the tension of separateness and identification at play. With the advancement in technology new communication platforms like new media and social media reflect well this human dilemma. The use of new technologies of communication has been blamed for the dearth of interpersonal interactions in families and among colleagues. People are glued to their electronic devices interacting with virtual friends miles away ignoring those physically around them. In families people chat less among themselves and spend much time surfing the internet and connecting with others on social media.

Platforms like LinkedIn or Facebook have groups that people who have something in common join. For instance, the alumni of University of Zambia would join a group on LinkedIn page hence, connecting by identification. In a way such individuals might have felt separated with their campus friends after graduation and the need to feel identified prompted them to find a space for interaction on LinkedIn or Facebook.

Creating a page of shared interest on social media is a way of naming the group through shared properties such as past associations or common interests, which are all shared identities. On LinkedIn there are a variety of groups of interests for instance, Old Munali Boys, Think Tanks, Chipolopolo Fans to name but a few. People who subscribe to these groups interact among themselves through blogs, post their profiles, find resources for jobs and access a variety of articles addressing pertinent issues in their area of interest.

These social identities on social media follow the hierarchical organization of society according to identification. If you do not share the same interests with other members on the social media you will automatically feel isolated. This isolation becomes pronounced when one realizes that he cannot speak the same language others are using on the platform. Each social cohesion has a language that bonds its members together. For instance, those in the medical field would tend to use jargon known to themselves and senseless to lay people. For those in the click this language becomes a vehicle for identification and for a layperson a tool for alienation hence, the process of associating and disassociating with others.

New media and social media meet the end result of identification in many ways. The end result of communication is actually the very aim of communication. When individuals create social cohesion through Facebook or LinkedIn they manage to have their needs satisfied. For instance, if one joins the Facebook group page of University of Zambia alumni the reasons for joining would be to be part of a network of friends that can support each other. Through this platform alumni can find connections to new careers, they might also get clients to their business, and others might also find future partners in marriage or business. The needs of members to a particular group on social media may vary according to individuals' interest. Others might use this platform for socialization purposes while others might use it for serious business networking and the like. The interests and needs met on the social media are what would be termed as the end result of identification.

New media and social media are tools that help humanity extend itself and communicate with a new language. In as much as it is seen to disconnect people from interpersonal interactions it also connects and expands human interactions defying the odds of distance and proximity. Burke's concept of separateness and identification plays well in the world of new media and social media. It is incumbent upon humanity to explore more of this new reality and make new media and social media meet the needs and interests of people who discover their identification on these platforms.

Questions for reflection:

1. Should social networks and online publications be regulated like broadcasting? Why and why not?
2. Is it true that social media liberates us and at the same time alienates us being present and available to those near us?
3. What are the merits and demerits of new media and social networks?

Chapter Ten

ICT Power to the People

In the recent past the Zambian media landscape has been evolving in all aspects and dimensions. The Public's broad sheets and private tabloids newspapers have not yielded to the annals of history neither have the terrestrial television and radio broadcasting. The mainstream newspapers, instead have seized the opportunity and maintained or assumed their presence online; the new platform. New tabloids have emerged in both formats (print & online). Online publications have also multiplied. The level of utilizing interactive media for intellectual intercourse has been wanting. Most bloggers on a number of these online publications lack the intellectual sting as they only trade insults to each other. Many fail to identify issues from the media and subject such to critical analysis but instead they focus and attack the person. Perhaps, this is a new culture eroding our nation, as it is also apparent in the political arena.

Apparently, Television broadcasting is moving, on a snail pace though, to digitalization. Internet wise, the fiber optic generation has not fully stamped its head, as Internet access, in Zambia, is still a daunting nightmare. We need to feel the benefits of Independent Broadcasting Authority bill (IBA) and Zambia Media Ethics Committee (ZAMEC). We are in the digital age and as Zambians there is no reason to linger behind when Internet access is an outright human right issue (Freedom of Information). The Freedom of Information bill (FOI) or the Access to Information bill (ATI) should urgently be enacted into law. The media terrain must be exciting though still bristly.

It was always thought that the mainstream publications would slowly fold-up with the emerging new media platforms. It has indeed been witnessed in the west were print publications have been replaced by online publications. Even in broadcasting few people would listen to radio or watch television where by everyone is listening or watching the same thing on a national broadcaster.

People read news; listen to music and watch electronic footage streamed on their gargets and social media platforms. Some countries in Africa have also caught up with this advancement in technology. In Zambia are we there? Quite right cable television like Digital Satellite Tele Vision (DSTV) has brought us closer to technology but still can we access electronic content through our gargets like mobile phone, tablets, iPads, iPods and the like when internet access and bundles are expensive and erratic. Nearly every Zambian has a cellphone but how reliable are the network service providers with their networks?

If Zambia Information and Communications Technology Authority (ZICTA) gained greater autonomy with the passage of the ICT Act, why has other players not emerged to showcase the liberalization of the fixed market and international gateways? Vodacom is one of the cheapest network providers winning the African market but why is Zambia reluctant to bring in more players to enhance competition, which will bring down the cost of communication? Poor and expensive Internet is blamed on inadequate international communications infrastructure due to the fact that Zambia is a landlocked country and it relies heavily on the neighbouring countries for interconnections and also on satellite links. The ICT Act which was adopted by government in 2006 set priorities areas of which ICT development was one of them with its 13 pillars like developing a competitive local ICT industry, increasing access to ICT services, expanding the national backbone, creating an enabling framework for competitive converged telecoms/ICTs and many others related to education, health and agriculture. The paranoia by local ICT providers of multinationals who rejoice in the higher consumer rates for their self-aggrandizement is the sure cause of underdevelopment in the ICT in Zambia. A developed ICT in Zambia as envisioned in the ICT policy and its strategies would surely yield ripple effects not only to the ICT consumer but also to the development of the nation as whole. Information is power and if in this fast-paced technological epoch people are denied this right then they will remain disempowered.

Think of any industry now, you will realize that it has been impacted by technological innovations. How many millions of kwacha are we losing in this country with our archaic and none conversional ways of doing things? In this world time counts and matters, as every minute wasted costs money. Other countries are moving ahead and matching up with ICT innovations while we sit on our policies and do the unproductive palaver. ICT ought to be a priority if we have to make inroads in development as a nation because it cuts through all areas of productivity like agriculture, education, health, infrastructure and communication.

When Marshall McLuhan envisaged the global village he had an intuition of how communication technology would connect the universe though he himself lived in an age that media had not yet fully budded. We as a nation deserve an equal share of the benefits and the feel of what this global village is and this can be ascertained only through easy and cheaper access to new platforms of knowledge and creativity. It's high time ZICTA saw to it that the ICT Act was resuscitated and ignited after its proverbial stillbirth. The FOI, once enacted into law, IBA and ZAMEC should not be white elephants but instruments and institutions that would chatter a new path in the media landscape of our nation.

The benefits of ICTs should be surely a shared Zambian dream that will open doors to new ways of governing, doing business, studying, and communicating. A farmer in Shang'ombo, Katete, Kasempa, Kalomo and many other places should find it easy to solve his/her daily farming puzzles by the click of a mouse. A teacher should be able to develop himself/herself and his pupils through easy access to the Internet for research. Our able doctors should be able to engage new technologies here in Zambia to accomplish their medical tasks instead of doing it in foreign lands. Faster and cheaper Internet would be a great resource to the advancement of our higher learning institutions where libraries are known as places to slumber due to insufficient books and online database.

In the triangle of ICT it is the consumer that seems to be affected while the policy makers and providers evade surmountable challenges for supposedly vested interest. Meetings, conferences ought to bring measurable and realistic results for the consumer thereby empowering him/her.

Questions for reflection:

1. Why is access to information a human right issue?
2. What is your take on expensive Internet and lack of competition for network providers?

Chapter Eleven
The Leader you can become

Many people are poor leaders because they lack models to coach them or inspire them. Leadership is not about having a position or role of authority but it is about a person's ability to influence others whatever the situation or place in the organization or society. Not all people with positions of authority are leaders. We have all heard of this hypothetical question that: Are leaders born or made? Well, according to experts in leaderships this question can be answered by what they call the 30/70 rule, which holds that 30 % of leaders are born and 70 % of leaders are made. That is why it is possible for most of us to be formed as leaders.

Most of us when we think of models for leadership we think of big names like Kenneth Kaunda, Nelson Mandela, Mother Theresa, Martin Luther King, Mahatma Gandhi and so on. None of us would think of our own siblings, colleagues, teachers, clergy and others in society, who have influenced us in one way or the other. If you think seriously you would realize that you are where you are not because of these big names but because someone simple like your mother or father committed herself by sacrificing that you go to school and become independent. There are many stories of people whose parents were simple people but who inspired their children to greater heights. If you are successful you may want to find out what made you succeed. Perhaps it is the little words your parents were telling you that gave you the strength or their industriousness that inspired you to put in your best.

One of the contemporary prophets in his preaching was asking pastors why their churches were not growing and he told them that because they did not want to be under someone. They wanted to be bosses and manage their own affairs. That strategy would not yield any positive results. Why do sports men and women have coaches? It is because it is always important to have an expert to provide us with challenges. Having a coach provides us with an opportunity to see what others are doing and to get necessary information that would help develop. The coach is there to help you practice well and because he is an outsider he/she is able to see your progress and compare that to what he/she knows.

Practicing is essential but practicing under a coach or expert multiplies the end results. That is why it is necessary to identify someone in your field who has expertise so that you work under him/her and come to learn how to do things. Chess is believed to be a game of the elite in the intellectual realm but in Uganda a little girl from the slam, Yohana Mutesi, defied the odds by storming at a mission to search for something to eat and found that a Uganda man, Robert Katende was offering porridge in exchange for playing chase. Yohana with no formal education was coached by Robert an expert and within a couple weeks she could beat her mentor and others at the game. Her mentor confessed that Yohana's skills in chess were extraordinary and mostly natural. Not long ago this teenager, Yohana rose to international stardom beating others in the game and winning Woman Candidate Master at the 40th Chess Olympiad and became the first youngest winner of the African Chess Championship.

Many people are failures in leadership because they have no one who inspires them or because they align themselves with poor coaches. When I wanted to become a teacher I was inspired by someone and also I realized that my classmates would come to me to teach them arithmetic. In my high school days I was coaching juniors and this time as a lecturer my students would find it easy to approach me and to ask for assistance. As a man of the cloth also I had seen preachers and priests who inspired me by their way of life and I wanted to be like them. I mingled with them, asked them difficult questions. As a journalist Zambian journalists like the late Jowi Mwiinga inspired me. *The Post Newspapers* was born when I was in high school at Munali and I used to enjoy reading political columns by Mwiinga. When later I went to a teacher training college I was in the writers club and was constantly writing for the college notice board. This helped me to hone my writing skills. Some years back I was able to win a national quiz organized by the civic education organization because I had practiced and I had models to learn from. We never cease to learn as people as every day is a learning opportunity. Therefore, we can only cultivate good leadership habits by willing to learn from those who have treaded the path we are treading in now. Pride will only leave us as dreamers who never realized their dreams.

Most of the people I have made reference to as my mentors were not in positions of leadership but they had authority. Our own peers can have an influence on us. Who are the people around us we admire who can influence us? The former Zambian minister of defense Godfrey Mwamba confessed once that he has been successful because of his dear mother whom he was feared, yet she inspired him to work harder. He said he is an example of someone who has made it in business not because of academic degrees but because he was disciplined.

Yes, formal education is necessary but not a guarantee for success. Many successful people in the world were failures academically. Bill Gates in 1975 never had a degree in information technology but he went on and established Microsoft. George Bush junior was a 'C' student but he became president of the United States. South Africa's retired Anglican archbishop of Cape Town, Desmond Tutu was also a 2/2 student but today he is worldly known for his stance on apartheid and other forms of discrimination as South African social activist. He also received the noble peace prize. Jacob Zuma in South Africa never went through formal education but made it in politics because he was able to position himself with successful people through networking and forming relationships.

Many people in governments and the corporate world are more managers than leaders and as a result they fail to inspire people or win trust of those they lead. Gifted leaders are not afraid to empower others because they are not insecure. Such leaders know that they become effective if they make things work out through others. They know how to delegate and build trust in others because they are very apt in sharing their vision and bringing others on board. They empower others because they too were empowered and because they learned their skills through being coached or mentored by experts in the field and also by deliberate practice. Never be deceived by thinking you can make it alone. No we need others in order to be sharpened and developed. We all have the potential for greater things if we are better disposed and put our whole self into it. The African adage "I am because we are." is true when it comes to human interdependence.

Questions for reflection:

1. What is the difference between a leader and a manager?
2. Does one need positional power to be a leader?

Chapter Twelve
We Need a Robust African Think-Tank

I hate Afro-pessimism because I believe Africa and Africans have the potential to succeed. It is high time as Africans we started believing in ourselves and in our own smaller ways make positive contributions to the developed of our continent. There are many Africans that are high profile intellectuals, professionals, strategists and ordinary folks that are changing the way of doing business in Africa and in diaspora. Many African doctors, engineers, entrepreneurs, academicians and social activists have opted to remain and work in their own countries with the aim of making a difference. In some parts of African these brave men and women work under unfavourable working conditions, usually poorly paid and sometimes without proper facilities. These men and women work with little notice or publicity. Others have opted to employ their expertise elsewhere where they think their services would reap better remunerations and offer proper working facilities. Despite the efforts of those who have opted to stay some Africans still fail to appreciate the services and expertise of these gallant sons and daughters of Africa who have opted to stay. They would rather seek similar services abroad. Sometimes the irony is that they might find that an African actually is attending to them in diaspora. Where is the problem?

It is always inspiring to see one return to his/her native country, after pursuing higher education elsewhere, with a desire to make a positive contribution and inspire changes. I remember some years back meeting a Zambian surgeon who had completed his masters degree at the University of Cape Town and had many offers to remain in South Africa but the man turned down the attractive offers and opted to return to Zambia and work at University Teaching Hospital. Since then the man has continued to do wonders in his practice because of his patriotism. Of course there are also some Africans who have a laissez faire attitude towards work and they do not inspire. These are the ones tarnishing the image of the African professionals. Most people in society notice these professionals, not interested in their country, and then portion the blame on every professional in the related field. Just like in our colleges there are many students who put in their best in studies and there are those who are lazy.

One of my logic professors from the University of Zimbabwe would argue that if you want to hide anything from an African put it in a book. Another classmate of mine used to argue also that if you moved all the Africans to the developed world and brought those from the developed world to Africa, the Africans would make the developed world deteriorate within a short time. The professor was expressing the dearth of a reading culture in Africa. My classmate's conclusion stems from the experience of Africa as a failed continent. Africa's failures are usually blamed on the colonial history despite self-rule for almost half a century. But are the two observations by my academic colleges a reflection of the state of affair of the Africa mind and spirit? There is good that can come out of Africans and Africa and I refuse to be identified by such demeaning sentiments. So does every African who has a sense of self-efficacy and determinism.

We need a robust African think-tank not only to overturn the mindset of some Africans who are Afro-pessimistic but also to reclaim the pride of the African intelligentsia. Firstly, we need to promote a reading and writing culture. History is very important and we ought to write our own history. Africans are said to have a depository of their culture through stories, songs and sayings. Ours is a narrative culture yet it is important to document our narratives for posterity. Some years back while teaching literature to a new class of grade tens, I asked my students what books they had read on their own in the past and I was taken aback to realize that none of them had actually read a novel. How many of us care to read a manual or conditions stipulated on documents that require our signatures? Why do people steal iron bars and stone placards for street names? Who cares to buy a map for a city or town? Can you even find them anywhere in Zambia? Where are our geography and history graduates to document these things?

One day I was asked by a colleague to give a short introduction of Zambia to a group of his Irish partners visiting Zambia. When I went on the Internet to compare notes I couldn't find anything written by a Zambian. Westerners did all the contributions, on the history of Zambia, posted on Google. I am talking about credible documentation, which has been as a result of thorough research, and not mere rumour.

Investing in research helps the nation to plan well because it has right information from which it can make informed projections into the future. It is the duty of public institutions of higher learning to invest in research thereby transforming themselves into institutions that have relevance to their communities. The design of the research projects for public institutions should be such that they generate knowledge that deals with real-life issues. What I am suggesting here is having robust think tanks in our institutions that would change the curriculum in our learning institutions to fit with the needs of our people. This would lead to the idea of Africa's commitment to mitigate its own challenges and providing relevant and meaningful solutions for its own betterment.

We need to develop a desire to know more about our own African cultures and history. The composition of African think tanks should not only be confined to academicians but also to artists such as musicians, poets, novelists and comedians. It could also include journalists, politicians, medical practitioners and all relevant professionals. The wisdom of ordinary Africans should be documented. Hence, it provides a body of knowledge and philosophy that could be consulted by future generations.

For international purposes we need to promote standards and high quality of our products and take pride in African products. It is disheartening to find an African who wants to mimic and imitate western culture at the detriment of Africa's own culture. The Chinese and Indians are advancing in all spheres because they believe in themselves. China's own online shopping is more popular than Amazon in China for the Chinese market because the ethos of China is different from those of the West. No wonder Amazon failed to break through this market. This matters more for China because the Chinese market is five times bigger than that of the United States. Nigerian, Kenyan and South African markets are also huge. Therefore, it is upon strategists to see to it that local investments capitalize of local consumers. This explains why these countries have made in-roads in literature, arts, and film in other parts of Africa. It would be interesting for instance to have a Zambian food chain or retail win the Zambian market. If these other African countries have done it because of patriotism other African countries could do it also. This is a great sign of Africa's renaissance.

Questions for reflection:

1. What is the role of the African intelligentia vis-à-vis Africa's development?
2. What is the place of the African artist in awakening consciousness of the African heritage, sage and culture?
3. Do you think we have original African innovators and enterpreneurs or we are just dependent on the developed world?

Chapter Thirteen
Oil Production and the future of Africa

Oil Production in Africa

It is often surprising to learn that some countries in Africa have oil deposits yet the local people in the areas of these resources languish in abject penury. Africa shares about 10 percent of the world deposits of oil while the Middle East has the highest oil deposits of 62 percent. If the very people living within the areas where oil deposits are found are not benefiting them, then there must be something wrong somewhere. The irony even becomes worse when there are long queues for petrol or diesel in some Africa's rich-oil countries.

Some year back I was reading online-news about my country Zambia and I came across an article entitled "State scouts for oil explorers." With the prospects of oil and gas discoveries, that seemed like good news for the copper rich nation. If the discovery becomes successful we could only hope that this would increase government revenue and create more jobs. It is not as easy as that as this could also mean disaster. Probably, with the discoveries then we might start fighting among ourselves with rebel groups emerging, oil companies and rich nations profiting while stirring the confusion as witnessed in other oil rich nations on the African continent and elsewhere.

Africa has oil deposits in countries such as Libya, Equatorial Guinea, Chad, South Sudan, Angola, Nigeria, Algeria, Egypt, Gabon and Congo Brazzaville. African oil deposits are of high quality with low sulfur content that requires little refining to get it to the pump. Hence, African oil is cheap, safe and more accessible. Apparently, African nations allow oil companies to their fields because there are no indigenous African oil majors. Since African states with oil deposits are only exporters then the importing nations through international oil companies benefit more than the actual people who live in the areas where oil is being mined. The local people in the oil rich areas are often displaced, killed or abused.

Nigeria and the conflict of Oil deposits

Most conflicts on the African continent could be attributed to the power struggle to control the oil exploration; exploitation and export by governments, rebel groups, international oil companies and individuals with resources. Take for instance the Niger Delta in Nigeria; the tribes in the area are struggling to survive. In June 2009 the Nigerian government extended an olive branch to the rebel groups causing havoc in the Niger Delta region in the quest to bring peace to this oil rich area. Since 1965 Nigeria has earned US$ 350 billion in oil revenues. Annually 76 percent of Nigeria's government revenue is from oil. You have companies like Shell, Total, Statiol, Chevron, ExxonMobil, Agrip exploiting the oils in the country.

Despite the huge number of oil companies operating in Nigeria oil smuggling is a reality. Due to illegal "bunkering" Nigeria is loosing billions of dollars every year. The late and former Nigerian President Umaru Yar'Adua once pleaded with oil importing nations in the international community to shun trading oil deals with corrupt suppliers in the trade he termed as "Blood Oil" equating it to "Blood Diamond" trade that had fuelled most civil wars in West African countries like Liberia and Sierra Leone. With all the riches in crude oil and the revenues accrued from it Nigeria surprisingly ranks 158 out of 177 countries on the United Nations' (UN) Human Development Index with 60 percent of its people living on less than US$1 a day.

Oil and Politics of Sudan

Sudan before separation, was the largest country on the African continent covering an area of about 2, 5 million Km square and a population of about 39, 3 million people and was the fifth African oil producing nation. Oil was seen as the principle factor in the politics of Sudan. Oil was the government's source of income as it accounted for about 92, 6 percent of export value. The oil industry in Sudan was poorly managed, and it was highly politicized. Oil production started with the construction of the first pipeline from the Southern Oil fields to the Red Sea in 1999. With this development there were conflicts within the oil areas, which caused hardships for the civilian population who were looted, displaced and killed by the thousands. When people were driven out from their land in a merciless campaign to assure safety of the oil industry the government and oil companies hypocritically presented the catastrophe as inter-tribal clashes; a continuation of traditional strife.

When the international community imposed sanctions on Sudan, the US government prohibited US companies from doing any business in Sudan, except in the oil-rich Southern part. In the Comprehensive Peace Agreement (CPA) of January 2005 the government of Sudan accepted that it would lose its exclusive military control over the oil fields by 2007. Also the Sudanese People's Liberation Movement/Army (SPLM/A); ruling the South, agreed that the national government was entitled to 50 percent of revenues of the oil produced in the South. Eight European NGOs established the European Coalition on Oil in Sudan (ECOS) in 2000. Its aim was to advocate for action by government and the business sector to ensure that Sudan's oil wealth contributes to the peace and equitable development. By 2009 Sudan ranked 147 out of 177 countries on the Human Development Index.

The biggest investors in South Sudan oil are China, Malaysia and India. China National Petroleum Company (CNPC) is Southern Sudan's leading oil company. Chinese investments in Southern Sudan are in excess of US$6 billion, predominantly in the oil industry. Malaysia's state oil firm Petronas alone has investments worth $1, 45 billion in Sudan.

Libya Oil Industry

Libya has the highest oil reserves in Africa and the oil industry accounts for 90 percent of national exports earnings and approximately 30 percent of Gross Domestic Product (GDP). The National Oil Corporation (NOD) is the largest oil company in Libya. Libya's oil has been under-explored due to the sanctions which where imposed on Libya by the UN and USA in 1992 and the stringent fiscal terms Libya imposed on foreign oil companies. The UN and USA lifted the sanctions in 2003 and 2004 respectively. With this development oil majors have stepped up exploration efforts for oil and gas. The biggest importers of Libya's oil are found in Europe; most Italy and Germany. Libya; a country covering an area of 1,759,540 square kilometers with a population of about 5,5 million people, ranks 56 out of 177 countries on the Human Development Index; a position higher than a couple of years ago. Libya, a medium rich nation has low illiteracy levels; a sign that its riches are benefiting its people. This is a scenario expected to materialize in the other oil-rich African countries.

China Oil Investments in Africa

Africa might have these many oil deposits, yet it is not the biggest consumer. United States of America is the world biggest consumer of oil followed by China, European Union and Japan. In the recent past global demands of energy has increased. Conventional oil reserves reaching their peak production, oil companies looking for new opportunities are tapping into Africa's growing oil industry.

With the booming economy China requires massive levels of energy to sustain it. China gets one third of its oil imports from Africa with 60 percent of this coming from Sudan. The main suppliers of oil to China in Africa are Angola, Republic of Congo, Equatorial Guinea and Sudan. The West often views Chinese investment in Africa with suspicion. In trading with Africa, China offers integrated packages of aid to Africa and often assumes a noninterference in domestic affairs. It is often said that China does not mix business with politics but this is contestable in that China provides military support and sells arms to Sudan. Though China is often demonized by the West because of engaging despotic regimes on the African continent and on other human rights issues, the West and the U.S.A are not different either. China needs to improve in its trade with Africa by supporting local industries and revising its labour policy of 70 percent Chinese labour to employing more locals under good working conditions. Africa's turning towards China in trade, especially oil exploration and production, should be encouraged because China is a growing economy and well intentioned partner that supports developing nations in other areas such as education and infrastructure development.

Oil production hope for Africa

Though it is estimated that Africa's oil reserves accounts for 10 percent of the world oil production it is believed that Africa could have even more reserves to be explored. Currently, it is only a fraction of the African countries with oil reserves that experience conflicts. The majority of these countries; especial in North Africa, have stable governments and a thriving oil industry. Algeria, Egypt and Libya have vibrant economies a situation that enables the equitable distribution of the oil proceeds to its people through services. The GDP and literacy levels of these oil-rich nations are impressive. We could only hope that the militants and rebels groups that terrorize the Niger Delta area, South Sudan, Chad and other places with oil reserves would concede and let peace reign for better legal oil exploration, production and exportation. The other expectation is that Africa would begin having oil majors to even double its oil profits. The international oil majors should not only exploit African oil but also plough its profits back into Africa through providing aid and bursaries amidst spearheading community and infrastructure development. The future of Africa shines brighter with the exploration of more oil reserves.

Questions for reflection:

1. What do African countries with oil deposit need in order to remain peaceful and benefit from these resources?
2. Is blaming the developed world for the conflict of Africa justifiable?
3. If you were in charge of natural resources in your country what would you do to safeguard the interest of your nation rather than the interest of the investors?

Chapter Fourteen
Arms Trafficking

Arms trafficking a source of unending conflicts.

Every year the allotment for the ministry responsible for security and defense in the national budgets, for some countries in both the developed and the developing world, far exceed that of health, agriculture and tourism. One wonders why security and defense receives such huge budgetary allocations in some of these countries; even for peaceful nations that have no contemplation of ever engaging in war. Nations continue to acquire military equipment and weapons all in the guise of trying to establish peace and stability in the world. In recent years efforts and resources have been directed towards combating terrorism and above all to curtail the production of weapons of mass destruction. Yet, what has led to innumerable conflicts and loss of lives world over has been ignored; the arms trade. Without underestimating the dangers of weapons of mass destruction, in the world today, the biggest problem is actually the arms trade; especially small arms and light weapons, with all its ramifications.

Arms' trafficking has become a big and worrying business that the world can no longer ignore. The business surfaces in two forms; as legal trade and as illicit trade on the black market. Both the state sanctioned trade and the illicit trade in arms are causes to the irresponsible use of arms and the catastrophes that ensues. The illicit trade of small arms and light weapons is a world phenomenon. There are many factors that contribute to the existence of small arms and weak weapons in the hands of terrorists or wearing factions. International and national efforts are endlessly being made in order to mitigate the world's bloody conflicts that results due to the presence of arms and weapons. Who are really benefiting in the arms trade? The effects of arms trafficking cannot be under-estimated. One has just to look at the instability in Pakistan, Sudan, Colombia, Afghanistan, Chad, Guinea-Bissau and other war torn zones and realize that we are never safe. The world can no longer stand askew and watch these developing nations relegated to unruliness and mayhem while lucrative arms-barons siphon millions of dollars through arms trafficking.

Arms' trafficking has evolved into a phenomenon enterprise with big nations supplying arms and military associated weapons to many nations around the globe. The trade in arms and military associated machinery has benefited exporting nations while causing unbearable catastrophes on importing states, which are mostly developing nations and already impoverished. Most conflicts in the world are perpetuated due to the trade in arms.

Illicit arms trade is a trans-national world syndicate fuelled by lack of strict international criteria and control. Arms brokers are able to operate because they circumvent national arms controls and international arms embargoes or obtain official protection. What is this business of arms trafficking all about? Illicit arms trade is the exchange of weapons for money, drugs and other commodities that crosses national boarders and spans the globe. Often, illicit arms trade involves small arms and light weapons such as machine guns, stinger missiles, rocket-propelled grenades and mortars. Illicit arms are weapon of choice in the majority of today's regional conflicts and many government armies, rebel forces and terrorist groups operating around the world. There is a predictable correlation between drug trafficking, corruption, oil trade, precious stones smuggling and arms trafficking. In these syndicates, sometimes, the profits realized from drug deals or diamonds or oil is used to acquire arms and weapons. Those who are involved in such transaction are always happy to keep the conflict alive. Corruption manifests itself when deals are struck to divert legally acquired arms into the hands of rebels and terrorists.

At most, illicit trade involves small arms and light weapons rather than the most dreaded weapons of mass distraction. Small arms and light weapons are easy to transport through boarders. Particularly, small arms are portable and easily concealed. They are designed for personal use; several people design light weapons for use. Small arms include revolvers and self-loading pistols, rifles and carbines, sub machine guns, assault rifles, and light machine guns. Light weapons includes heavy machine guns, grenades launchers, portable anti-aircraft and anti-taker guns, recoilless rifles, portable launchers of anti-tanker missiles, rocket systems, and anti-aircraft missile systems, mortars of calibres of less than 100mm, ammunition, shells, and missiles for the above; grenades; landmines; and explosive. Heavy weapons include all conventional military equipment such as tanks, armoured vehicles, military helicopters, fighter aircrafts, artillery guns, rocket launchers and mortars with calibres greater than 100mm.

According to the International Institute for Strategic Studies report (October, 2008); the world military expenditure in 2007 is estimated to have reached $1,339 trillion in current dollars. This represents a 6 percent increase in real terms since 2006 and 45 percent increase over the 10-year period since 1998. The USA, responsible for about 80 percent of the increase in 2005, is the principle determinant of the current world trend, and its military expenditure now accounts for just under half of the world total, at 45 percent of the world total for the larger arms purchasing nations each year. Arms procurement is 20 – 30 percent of their military budgets. Arms procurement is normally operations, maintenance and personnel. Some 40 – 50 billion dollars are in actual deliveries. Each year, around 30 – 35 billion dollars are made in actual sales (agreements or signing of contracts).

The Stockholm report of 2008 revealed that; developing nations continue to be the primary focus of foreign arms sales activities by weapons suppliers. Major purchases continue to be made by a select few developing nations in these regions, principally China and India in Asia, and Saudi Arabia in Middle East. The strength of individual economies of a wide range of nations in the developing world continues to be a significant factor in the timing of many of their arms purchasing decisions. Increases in the price of oil, while an advantage for major oil producing states in funding their army purchasing has, simultaneously, caused economic difficulties. A number of less affluent developing nations have chosen to upgrade while reducing new purchases.

Small-arms:

The growing availability of small arms has been a major factor in the increase in the number of conflicts, and in hindering smoother rebuilding of states and development after a conflict has ended. It is estimated, for example, that: there are around half a billion military small arms around the world. Civilians are affected mostly by small arms. Modern conflicts claim an estimated 500,000 people each year. 300, 000 of these are from conflicts, and 200, 000 are from homicides and suicides. 90 percent of civilian-casualties are caused by small arms. This is far higher than the casualty count from conventional weapons of war like tanks, bomber jets or warships. Estimates of the black market trade in small arms range from US$ 2-10 billion a year.

It is estimated that there are 639 million small arms and light-weapons and 16 billion rounds of ammunition in circulation worldwide produced by more than 1,135 companies in at least 98 countries. Eight million new weapons are produced every year. About 80 percent of small arms are in the hands of civilians. Every minute, a gun kills someone. It is estimated that the total number of military ammunition produced equal more than two military bullets for every man, woman, and child on the planet. Small arms are so prevalent that it is estimated that there is one such weapon for every 10 people – men, women and children- in the world. For instance, in Pakistan there is a gun for every 6 people and in Bangladesh there is a gun to every 180 people (Small Arms Survey 2001). Small arms and light weapons account for an estimated 60-90% of the 100,000+ conflict death each year and tens of thousands of additional deaths outside of war zone (Small arms survey 2005). In reality globally there are more guns being held by civilians than governments and police.

It is believed that "illicit drugs production thrives on territory outside the control of recognized governments, and 95 percent of the world's production of hard drugs takes place in the context of armed conflict. Armed groups illegally exploit valuable natural resources and their state sponsors, ruining millions of lives and impending local development. International trade suffers and illicit markets thrive, to the detriment of national economies" (Control Arms, 2005)

Suppliers-of-arms

Ordinarily, arms trade go on between nations as legal trade conforming to the international and national laws of both the importing and the exporting nations. At most, illicit arms trafficking goes on between individuals, groups and sometimes states through diversion of international and national laws or by not conforming to humanitarian and human right laws. Arms trade; be it legal or illicit, help prolong conflicts in most parts of the world.

Lack of stringent regulations and laws both at the international and national levels lead to some crooked tycoons, groups and individuals benefit from the trade while an enormous segment of the human species suffer its effects. Guns and rocket launchers are not manufactured to kill animals in the bush or to shoot stars in the air but to kill innocent human beings in Afghanistan, Darfur, Kabul, Kisangani, Bujumbura and everywhere. Guns are manufactured for unscrupulous people to murder and take innocent lives in the streets of our cities like Nairobi, London and Johannesburg and in the classrooms of New York and California. The world's efforts should not be laid only on the need to control weapons of mass destruction ignoring the trade in conventional weapons that operate in a legal and moral vacuum.

United Kingdom and France in 1998 to 2001 earned more income from arms sales to developing countries than they gave in aid. United States, UK, France, Russia, and China are the big five in the world's arms trade. These countries together are in charge of 88 percent of conventional arms exports. The USA alone exports about 45 percent of all the world's exported weapons. These permanent members of the UN Security Council are deeply entrenched and profit from the arms trade. Other countries that have been involved in supplying arms to other nations are countries such as Albania, Egypt, North Korea, Bulgaria and Slovakia. Companies like Heckler & Koch; the world's second-largest manufacturer of small arms, have sold weapons to repressive regimes in Burma and Indonesia, trafficked into war-zones in Bosnia and Darfur.

It is estimated that 25 and 30 non-state groups spread throughout the world possess shoulder-fired missiles and small arms. Small arms and light-weapon are preferred because they are cheap, widely available, lethal, simple to use, durable, portable, concealable, make it easy to cross borders and has; at most, legitimate uses.

Finland is a major arms trading partner with Israel. Since 2002, the value of trade between Finland and Israel in anti-tank guide missiles has been more than 4 million Euros. North Korea's arms trade has focused on Iran, Syria and Libya. North Korea's arms have been sold to Egypt, Pakistan and the military regime in Myanmar. Sales of short-and-medium-range missile systems remain among North Korea's largest export earners generating closer to US$1.5 billion annually. The country's weapon industry has played a crucial role in the spread of ballistic-missile capabilities across the Middle East in recent decades.

Why small arms and light weapons end up in wrong hands:

There are a number of factors that lead to small arms and light-weapons ending up in wrong hands of terrorists, rebels, pirates, bandits or individuals. For instance, the discontinuation of apartheid in South Africa, the end of conflict in Mozambique; Sierra Leone; Liberia and Angola resulted in small-arms ending up in the hands of criminals that everyday mug and murder innocent human beings. Also the accessibility of arms to civilians in some of these countries has lead to unimaginable-armed violence in homes and slams. Somalia is an example of the dangers of light weapons proliferation and irresponsible arming of unstable regimes by former powers. Hundreds of thousands of small arms in leaky government arsenals are vulnerable to theft, loss and diversion. For instance, in 2001, traffickers acquired 5,000 AK-47 from Yugoslavia army stock and moved from Serbia to Liberia under the guise of a legal transaction with Nigeria. Another instance is that of West Africa where gun smugglers persuaded the Nicaraguan government to sell 3,000 assault rifles and 2.5 million rounds of ammunition by pretending to be brokering the deal on behalf of the Panamanian National Police. In the process the illegal goods where directed to South America and sold to an international terrorist organisation known as the United Self-Defense Forces of Columbia.

In countries were military personnel have not been paid; soldiers might sell the weapons for cash. Sometimes, soldiers have sympathized to a rebel causes and sell weapons for cash. Also weapons are often stolen from both legitimate and illegal civilian owners. Small-scale burglary alone enables half a million U.S. weapons to enter the black market every year. In order to keep supplies flowing the manufacturers and the exporting states see to it that their products are utilized to the maximum. The more conflicts there are the more profit the manufacturers and suppliers make. In 2001 the USA offered the government of Philippines military equipment worth more than US$100 million- including helicopters and transport planes and 30,000 M16 rifles – to fight various armed groups. The transfers were agreed as part of USA 'war on terror.'

Why is it problematic to end manufacturing of arms and later on the trade itself?

Why is it difficult to stem the flow of small arms and light weapons? These weapons have legitimate military, law enforcement, sporting and recreational uses. These uses interdict the type of outright bans on manufacture, stockpiling and sales imposed on landmines and chemical and biological weapons. What governments try to do is to prevent the diversion and misuse of these weapons without unduly infringing upon legitimate use and trade. Actually, others might think arms trafficking is not an easy problem to solve but a problem to manage. Is it really? This problem can be solved like many other world problems.

According to the Stockholm report 90 percent of international air cargo carriers; named in the UN Security Council report and other arms trafficking reports, have also been used by UN agencies, EU and NATO governments, leading NGOs and private contractors. It is noted that in some cases air cargo companies deliver both aid and weapons to the same conflict zone.

International efforts to mitigate arms trafficking

Why should the world get concerned about arms trade and in particular illicit arms trafficking? The United Nations in 2001 came up with a programme of action to prevent, combat and eradicate the illicit trade in small arms and light weapons when it convened in New York. The participating states were gravely concerned about the manufacturing, transfer and circulation of small arms and light weapons. Much more, they were concerned about the excessive accumulation and uncontrolled arms trafficking spread of small arms and light weapons in many regions. They saw that these negative developments have a wider range of humanitarian and socio-economic consequences and pose a serious threat to peace, reconciliation, safety, security, stability and sustainable development at the individual, local, national, regional and international levels. They realized that small arms and light weapons in the hands of terrorist and criminals are a danger to society as they cause destabilization leading to failure of states and create the condition in which terrorist organizations emerge and thrive. Hence, they saw the need for a concerted effort in the project of managing arms trafficking. The UN recognized that arms trafficking exacerbate criminal violence, disrupt development efforts, and interfere with efforts to deliver humanitarian aid to victims of armed conflicts, feed the arsenals of world's worst terrorists, contribute to the displacement of civilians and undermine respect for humanitarian law. Misuse of arms jeopardizes people's fundamental rights, including right to life. Indirectly, it denies people access to socio-economic rights such as education, health, shelter and employment. The UN worked for the establishment of the Arms Trade Treaty (ATT).

The import and export of small arms were made illegal in 16 West African states in June 2006 when Ecowas adopted a landmark, binding convention on small arms, light weapons and other associated materials. Government representatives from 42 Africa countries agreed to sign an international treaty on banning cluster bombs. The African Union through NEPAD's peer review has also mechanisms to mobilize states in disarmament and non-proliferation of arms and weapons.

Focus on arms trafficking in Africa

Sadly, African continues to experience more armed conflicts than any other continent. Since it gained independence in 1975 Guinea-Bissau has been characterized by armed violence and instability. A country of only 36,120 square kilometers and a population of about 1.5 million people, Guinea-Bissau is regarded as one of the most impoverished nations in the world.

The result of protracted wars has led to an increase in the number of weapons in the country. It is estimated that there are 650,000 light-weapons and small arms in circulation in Guinea-Bissau alone. The widespread weapon possession among civilians is a fall-out from years of war. Other factors to the increase in weapon possession among civilians are lack of border control, weak rule of law and sub-regional allies that allow weapons to cross the border. There are up to 8 million light weapons currently in circulation in West Africa. Instability in Ivory Coast, Guinea, Mauritania, Chad and Sudan also contribute to the increase of weapons in Guinea-Bissau. It is alleged that elements in Guinea Bissau's military have supported the Separatist Movement of Democratic Forces in Cassamance- (Senegal) over the years. There have been accusations of the military smuggling weapons across the boarder. In the recent past there has been an increase in armed robberies, murders and theft of livestock. Farmers in southern Guinea-Bissau keep weapons to protect their livestock from a mounting problem of cattle rustling. More people are using weapons to steal cattle. The unstable environment has made Guinea-Bissau one of the West African countries that serve as an exchange point between Latin America and Europe for criminal groups that trade in drugs such as narcotics.

The government of Guinea-Bissau in March 2008 instituted the security sector reforms. A mandate to streamline and modernize the country's armed forces, police unity, air force, navy and judiciary. The government wants to take weapons out of some military as well as civilians. The programme under the security sector reform is to demobilize 2,500 members of its security forces. The programme has a budget of $183 million needed to carry out the expected reform. There has been fear in some quarters that the move to cut army manpower would have grave consequences. The Economic Community of West African States (Ecowas), international donors and UN peace building support office in Guinea-Bissau are supporting the reforms

In 2006 the government formed a committee against the proliferation of light weapons and small arms. The committee has drawn up a strategy to curb small arms, but it has just $60,000 to collect and destroy weapons. Foreign and Commonwealth Office (FCO) is helping by funding the programme to collect and destroy small and light-weapons and ammunition. So far it had given 14,975 pounds. The Cleared Ground Demining, a UK-based voluntary organization, runs the programme.

Guinea-Bissau's history has been littered by coups, counter-coups and other political violence, including the assassination of Army Chief of Staff Gen Tagma Na Wai and President Joao Bernardo Vieira and the murder, by the army over an attempted coup, of one of the presidential candidates, Baciro Dabo.

Elsewhere in Africa the story remains the same. There were about nine opposition groups in Sudan which included Beja Congress, Darfur Liberation Front (DLF), Democratic Unionist Party (DUP), Janjaweed, Justice and Equality Movement (JEM), National Alliance Forces (SAF), Sudan Liberation Army (SLA), Sudan Liberation Movement (SLM), and Sudan People's Liberation Army (SPLA) before the separation. Two main rebels groups in Sudan; the JEM and the Sudan Liberation Movement/Army (SLM/A) flared up a conflict with the government in 2003 over marginalization and distribution of wealth and power. This conflict has resulted in fighting between splinter rebel groups, increased banditry and ethnic clashes. The Darfur conflict pits mostly non-Arab rebels against the Arab-dominated government and has exacerbated tensions between nomadic Arabs and settled Black Africans in the region. While Black Africans have suffered most in the conflict, Arabs have also been victims.

The SPLM governs in the south. There have been numerous clashes between rival groups in the south, which have killed several hundred people. The SPLM and its National Democratic Alliance (NDA) allies have; in the past, received political, military and logistical support primarily from Ethiopia, Uganda and Eritrea. Uganda and Ethiopia have in the past supplied SPLM with arms and permission to train its forces within their territory. Eritrea allowed SAF to use its territory for training, and supports its activities.

Despite the Comprehensive Peace Agreement (CPA), which was signed in 2005 to end 21 years of civil war in Sudan, violence still persists. According to the UN estimation 300,000 people have been killed and another 2.7million continue to live in refuge camps in Sudan and neighbouring countries in a more than five years of fighting in Darfur, pitting rebels against Government forces and allied Janjaweed militiamen.

The north and south of Sudan are divided by ideological, cultural and religious differences over which the war was fought. The Sudanese government by then blamed Chad for supporting the anti-government rebel group the Justice and Equality Movement (JEM); Chad also accuses Sudan of sponsoring rebels there. In Somalia, a nation of about eight million people, it is estimated at least one million people have been internally displaced by almost perpetual civil conflict since the collapse of its central government in 1991. In Uganda, in 1991, one could purchase an AK-47 assault - rifle for a price of a chicken.

The Democratic Force for the Liberation of Rwanda (FDLR) is a Rwandan militia responsible for the 1994 Genocide against the Tutsi and has been in the DRC for the last 15 years from where they are accused of championing a humanitarian catastrophe. Countries such as Belgium, Germany, Israel, Spain, Albania, Romania, Slovakia and South Africa supplied arms and associated military equipment to the government of Rwanda, Uganda and Zimbabwe who participated in the Congo conflict. In the recent past, the African Union asked the international community for sanctions to be imposed on Eritrea for allegation that it was supplying arms to Somalia.

Africa has suffered the most due to the effects of the arms trafficking. The evils of this trade on the continent are vast and a source of worry. Greedy has made many individuals and terrorist groups acquire weapons and arms raping the continent of its natural resources while fanning wars and conflicts. The African Union (AU) through NEPAD peer review has tried to put in place mechanisms to manage the trade. If NEPAD fails to monitor and inspire more actions against arms proliferation then it would be true to conclude that this organ, and its parent AU, is a white elephant.

Questions for reflection:

1. Would you support gun ownership by civilians in your country?
2. Terrorists groups like Boko Haram cause mayhem in places like Nigeria and also the Al Qaeda in East Africa. Do you think their basis for attack is religious or such groups hide in the name of religion?

Chapter Fifteen
Models of a Free Media

In our world today calls for a free press have been raised constantly due to concerns about the political economy of communication. When we talk of political economy of the media we are overly concerned about how the media run and who has influence on the way the media operates. For instance, media houses in Zambia operate under a three-tier-system; that is state capital, corporate capital and community capital. It is obvious that state run media fall under state capital and are tools in the hands of the state or government to advance programming that promotes nationhood and development. One of the setbacks for the public media is that sometimes politicians utilize it as a propaganda tool. The corporate run media targets the market and treats its viewers or listeners or readers as consumers whom it should sell its product to. Community media can be varied and can be categorized within the realm of shared interest. Thus we might have religious community media or institutional community media, with each catering for the interest of its specific community. Given this background we can deduce that the debate for a free media is not an easy one. When we speak about a free media what are speaking about? When we envisage a free media what freedom are we advocating for? The media should be free from whom?

The public broadcaster in Zambia for instance has extended its antennas for revenue. Apart from government grants and the sell of advertisement slots it has added one baby to its wagon and that is the television taxes that viewers pay with their electricity bills. Moreover, it is called a broadcasting corporation unlike previously when it was known as a public service broadcaster. By broadening its revenue tentacles and assuming a corporate identity the public broadcaster has tried to move away from government control. By implication the public broadcaster should operate independently of state control. Its focus should be to serve the public interest and national interest. The same logic given for the public broadcaster could be extended to the other public media like radio, newspapers and the Internet.

The commercial media in an environment of competition has to package its products in such a way that it attracts the consumers. As it were, it is argued that commercial media houses have to give the consumers what they want. In the mind of the commercial media the readership, viewers or listeners are consumers and they ought to be served with advertisements. However, the irony is that the commercial media houses cannot package advertisement alone as an end products. They need to first attract the consumer with a bait of good soppies or movies, entertainment, sports, news, features, documentaries and the list is unending. Once a commercial television is known for good programming then it would win many viewers cum consumers. The same with a commercial radio that has good entertainment like music, drama, news and interviews, it would easily win many listeners cum consumers. So the story goes for a commercial newspaper that has well investigated news stories, and features and sports, it would easily widen its readership. The only setback for the commercial media house would be to solely regard and treat its readers or viewers or listeners as consumers and negate their right to information, entertainment and education. Another setback would be for the commercial media house to only propagate news stories that favours the vested interests of its financiers to the detriment of serving market and public interest.

Community media houses have a mandate to serve the interests of their particular communities of interest. Take for instance, a media product run by a university community should serve the interest of that community and doing so would be serving the public interest. A community radio station run by a religious institution should serve the interest of that particular religious community. The interest of a community can not only be limited to the immediate shared interest like education for a university run media house or religion for a religious run media house. Of course, the largest quota of programming should be in the shared interest of the community. We would expect a religious media house to have its primary focus on evangelization and the other interest should be secondary. Every community of shared interest should also have some interest in politics, entertainment and sports for it to be relevant to our world today. It should also promote human rights, concerns for the environment, gender, development and culture as these are interests that cut through race, age, religion, profession, class and the like. Also the interests of different age groups should be catered for in these media of community of interest.

When we speak of a free media we are talking of the media as one entity with a common aspiration to entertain, educate and inform. It is from this background that calls for a free media are made. It matters less whether the media are commercial, state or community run. The calls for a free media aspire for a free public and private media. To have a free media there are things that ought to be put in place. Firstly, the regulatory framework should be free from government and capital interference. That is to say there is need for an independent regulator and in some case the media houses should have some internal regulatory mechanisms as a social responsibility strategy. It is not only government interference that should be avoided but also capital interference. That is to say those who own media houses should let the media operate independently. A free media is desirable because the media ought to be the conscience of society. The media as the fourth estate means the media are part of the organ of state that has a mandate like the three organs of state. In a democratic dispensation, the media, civil society and government are partners in bringing about development and in the blossoming of the political systems like democracy itself.

Questions for reflection:

1. Do you think the media are free in most countries?
2. Are their models of media that are not biased?
3. What are the benefits of independent regulation for broadcasting against state regulation?

Chapter Sixteen
Story telling: Tell it like it is

Story telling is one of the principles that facilitates good communication and enhances connectivity to ones audience. It is one of the principles that have been effective for centuries in communication. Most cultures in the world believe in the story principle as far as making the message stick for years. For instance, the Japanese have been known as great storytellers and they use this technique even in marketing and advertisement. The Japanese are not the originators of story telling; even the Greek philosophers used stories to teach valuable concepts. Today we know about the classic works of great philosophers because their works were packaged and preserved in a narrative style, for instance, the works of Socrates, Plato, Aristotle and many others. Think of world religions like Judaism, Christianity, Islam, Buddhism, Hinduism, these religions preserved their core values and teachings as written narratives or stories. Nearly most of them have the narratives about the human origins told in a story form and this is the reason people are able to remember them.

Stories are easy to remember and they give life to concepts, ideas and teachings. Stories carry with them many features such as memories; emotions and proximity that help them stick. Story telling is effective as a principle in communication especially when it echoes what people know and are able to relate with. Jesus was known as a great storyteller because his stories had an impact on his audience.

Story telling is effective when it appeals to the emotions of the targeted audience or readers. For instance the story of the Good Samaritan in the bible is effective because Jesus applies his imagination in telling it and this would definitely capture the emotions of the targeted audience. He does not only tell this story by giving only facts but by using a parable to convey meaning. This technique of utilizing some figures of speech such as parable, metaphor, simile, hyperbole and the like creates an image in the mind of the targeted audience, hence taping on their emotions. The good Samaritan's story, too, uses figurative language which makes it interesting to follow because the images used resonates well with what the listeners know and are used to.

Stories are efficacies also because of proximity. Stories that have images, characters and language that the readers can not only identify with but also relate to very easily are effective in making ideas stick. Stories work very well just like songs. True stories about people do very well in teaching, preaching, promoting a brand and in any other forms of communication. People can recall a story being narrated hence very easy for them to believe it and its influence in relation to the brand being promoted. Commercials that are presented in story form are believable because they talk about what people know and this helps them appreciate what they do not know. Stories are not abstractions talking about things that are not there. Stories talk about real things in the world out there and because of that they have the power to make an impression on listeners.

Stories should be well told. The fact that a story uses material drawn from people's everyday life and experiences this makes it more acceptable and believable. What supports the principle of story telling is the value of truth. True stories make an impact and impression on people. A fake story always receives disapproval; hence people tend not to believe it. It is relaxing listening to a story than to something that is abstract. Abstract concepts are easily forgotten because people fail to make links or connect them with something they know or have seen. Stories are credible because they are concrete and talk about the day-to-day experiences of people. Not everyone is a good storyteller. Story telling is a skill and a gift.

The art of story telling has survived over centuries and even now people only pay much attention to something that grabs their attention. Stories have that power to grab the attention of many. What supports the story principle is the fact of the truth of the story, the techniques applied in telling the story, the nature of the story and also its aim.

The story principle is challenged when the story fails to remain faithful to the value of truth. A story, whether it is a real story or a fictitious one, should always aim to transmit the truth. A fictitious story should make claims that are verifiable about a teaching or a brand being promoted. Fictitious stories that promote concepts that embody the value of truth make people identify with them. This is so because they reflect what happens in society and the values that society tries to promote. The story principle is challenged when it is poorly told due to the applications of poor techniques. People switch off when the story is not interesting. An example of a poor story is one that lacks a structure. Stories that are packet with information sometimes are heavy to listen to. Stories should be packaged lightly like in the case of religious stories like the blind man and the elephant or the origin of humanity. Most religious stories have a structure and they are focused. The story principle is challenged when it is fragmented. A story should always contain the beginning, the middle and the end. Arrangement is important to achieving the desired effect.

Whatever, the aim of the story is the storyteller should remain faithful to it. If the aim of the story is to inform then the material and the technique should be such that they facilitate the achievement of that end. The aim of a story depends on the audience. There are stories that aim to inform, entertain and persuade. In communications the three aspects just mentioned should, at most, go together.

Stories work today just like they did in the ancient times. Even with the advancement of technology stories remain the best forms of communication. All around us people are using stories. It is stories that remind us of what we have to do. People who are respected in the world today are those who had a story to tell. Of late a Pakistan girl, Malala has captured the attention of the world because she has an inspiring story to tell about promoting girl-child's education in her country. It is because Malala is speaking about her own experience under the hands of the Taliban that she is able to win the sympathy, empathy and support of the world. Malala has given a face to the issue of girl-child education not only in Pakistan but also all over the world. Her story is an example of the power of the story principle.

Questions for reflection:

1. What do you think make stories stick than mere starting facts and theories?
2. Stories like songs enhance retention of principles learnt. Do you agree?

Chapter Seventeen

The Global Economic Recession and Africa

The recent global economic downturn has hit America and Europe exceedingly with millions of people loosing their jobs. Africa, as it were, might not have immediately felt the pitch directly. The financial crunch has been as a result of lack of ethical practice in the international financial systems where banking systems have encouraged the credit culture resulting in a culture of immoral opulence. The sirens of danger were blinking earlier before the crunch with the bursting of the house bubble in the United States in August 2007. Indirectly, Africa and the developing world have begun enduring the global recession heat especially with the dwindling international donor support, drop in export revenue, remittances and direct foreign investment. In the current global financial milieu the export markets for Africa have collapsed and foreign capital has been withdrawn.

The economic recession has drastic effect on the donor support Africa receives from the U.S and other developed world. During the Bush administration the allocation for global AIDS programmes and PEPFAR [the US President's Emergency Plan for AIDS Relief] in the U.S budget was higher than the Obama administration's pledge for 2010. President Obama during his campaign proposed allocation of US$7.5 billion a year to PEPFER's HIV/AIDS programmes, and $2.7 billion to the Global Fund to fight AIDS. Unfortunately, due to the recession, for 2010 the US government has allocated US$ 6 billion for PEPFAR's HIV/AIDs programmes and $900 million for the global fund to fight AIDS, TB and Malaria, far below what Obama had promised. The U.S being the highest contributor to the global AIDS fund its move means that there will be fewer funds to mitigate the scourge. African leaders made a commitment in 2001 to set aside 15 percent of their national expenditure towards health. Since then only a handful of the countries managed to honour the promise as other countries prioritized other projects instead of health. A random survey, on the national budgets of African countries, shows that the budget's allocation for defense far exceeds those of health and agriculture. Now with the new financial climate even those countries that kept the 15 percent pledge on health have started withdrawing. For instance, Botswana will not be able to include new patients in its free antiretroviral (ARVs) treatment programme from 2016 onwards. Also Tanzania announced a 25 percent cut of its annual HIV/AIDS budget.

The World Economic Forum convening in Cape Town recently heard that Africa would need $80 billions of annual investment on infrastructure to rise up as a competing partner on the global market. Making the report World Bank's Vice-President, Africa Region, and former Nigerian education minister, Obiageli Katryn Ezekwesili plainly confessed that Africa was not capable of mobilising such a huge sum of money. The implication of this is that Africa has to turn to the West for assistance. In the current global situation that would be one of the other hurdles Africa has to surmount.

Recently, the Jubilee Debt Campaign called for the immediate debt cancellation of US$400 billion for the developing countries. According to the then Nick Dearden, a Jubilee director based in London, this would enable the world's 100 poorest countries mitigate poverty and cushion the devastating effects of the global financial downtrend on their economies. For instance, with the collapse of the copper price and international investors evading large-scale infrastructural projects; Zambia's future is unpalatable. The International Labour Organisation in its report released on the World Day Against Child Labour (12 June) warned that poverty is going to increase in the developing countries with the decease in aid, remittances, export revenue and foreign direct investment. The same report alluded that with the financial squeeze more girls are going to be withdrawn from school to seek jobs. With these indicators African leaders need to awake from their slumber and get to work. In this crisis they should rise above personal greedy and self aggrandizement to serving angels that would bail-out the masses under indigence.

Across Africa governments are tightening their belts however some moves seem well intentioned yet practically closer to impossible to implement. Amidst, the country's worst recession and the global financial crunch South African

President Jacob Zuma in his first state of the nation address promised to create half a million jobs in six months. However, how the people's president, leading a country with a striking contrast in the socio-economic strata, was going to achieve this was little known. Yet it is a sign of bravely for a man with the people at heart. In Kenya the then Finance Minister Uhuru Kenyatta presented the most applauded budget in the country's history that had more to give than receive. Value added tax on most goods was slashed and cabinet ministers asked to remain with one government vehicle and surrender the extra vehicle which would later be sold and the revenue generated used for other noble purposes. With the Kenyan government revenue base trimmed the accomplishment of the budget's targets had to depend on local borrowing. With the world's economic-hurricane this was not going to be an easy task for the humane finance minister. At least, Kanyatta was walking the talk for others to emulate.

With the majority of Africans living in abject penury, walking the tighter rope should certainly begin from the top. Governments in Africa are called to more ethical practice in their spending than ever before. Cushioning some of the major local investments is a moral path to take in order to rescue more job loses. The lifting of value added tax on essential commodities and other goods would surely benefit the common man and woman in this time of 'Noah.' Much more prioritizing education, agriculture, health, tourism, infrastructure development and investment would lead to a better future for Africa. The pitch of the economic recession on the ordinary folk would be lethal if African governments fail to chip-in and redress the situation. It is time African governments stood up and refurbished their tented image of being corrupt and greedy to a modest livelihood that enables equal redistribution of national resources thereby ennobling the underprivileged.

Chapter Eighteen
The Nature of Travel Journalism

Travel journalism fits into the broader category of non-fiction writing and specifically narrative literal journalism. This is so because in both the form fundamentally work in the narrative mode. Robyn Davidson's "introduction" in *The Picador Book of Journeys* gives a salient definition of travel journalism that it is "a non-fiction work in which the author goes from point a to point b and tells us something about it" (2002: 3). However, it is problematic to literally categorize travel journalism or rather travel writing into a single genre that is unique and exclusive. Works of travel journalism take many forms and structures.

Travel journalism, just like narrative journalism, has similarities with works of fiction, at least in style. It could be concluded that some genre of travel journalism are works of 'facts in need of fiction.' J. Hartsock purports that literary journalism, of which travel journalism is part, takes on a fiction format, yet making a truth claim to phenomenal experience (1999). To put it plainly, travel journalism is factual accounts of events, observations, judgments and historical aspects that apply the techniques of fiction. It could be further stated that travel journalism blends together the need for objectivity and subjectivity. These qualities do not conclusively define travel journalism. Therefore, it is imperative to probe into the peculiarity of travel journalism and what really constitute travel journalism by engaging in a close comparative analysis on selected passages from the work of two travel writers; namely, Justin Fox and Paul Theroux.

Essay focus

Consequently, this essay shall examine Justin Fox's travel writings; "Doubling the wintry capes" and "Zimbabwe's Wild side," and then Paul

Theroux's pieces; "The trans Karoo Express to Cape Town" and "Blue train Blues." The thrust of examining these travel journalism texts is to identify what answers each of these writers give, implicitly and/or explicitly, to the question, 'what is travel journalism?' How does it differ from other kinds of journalism and non-fiction? What are the aims and specific preoccupations of travel journalism, and what, according to each writer, makes a prose text qualify as 'travel journalism?' Having shown how the writers treat these questions, the essay shall locate and discuss techniques of writing shown in the selected texts that are helpful and would be helpful to apply in constructing works of travel journalism. This last section shall make reference to my own works; current and future.

The essay's progression shall be arranged as per individual questions instead of the examination of one text after another. Hence, the set of questions addressed form headings through which the essay shall be arranged.

What is travel journalism?

Travel journalism takes many shapes but above all it has to involve some movement from; say, point A to point B as earlier noted by Davidson. Whilst the earliest genre of travel writings documented by Western civilizations, involved exploring the unknown territories, encountering other civilizations and penetrating the virgin lands in our age this is no longer the case. Davidson notes, "it is an irony that just when the ability to both travel and publish has penetrated the boundaries of class, race and sex, there should be nowhere left to discover" (6). With globalization the world has become a global village fusing all civilizations making what was seen as primitive civilizations a thing of the past. There is no place that has never been explored before and to write about such is to write about what the reader knows. It is this scenario that has transformed the perception of travel writing. In this new age travel journalism embraces both writing about foreign territories and writing about the local. Davidson captures this reality accurately when he notes that;

> Describing what lies beyond must be one of the oldest compulsions to story telling. Certainly it was already there at the inception of writing, and the prototype must have existed since human self-consciousness began. The metaphor of the journey is embedded in the very way in which we conceive of life – a movement from birth to death, from

this world to the next, from ignorance to wisdom. In the Aboriginal philosophy, its metaphorical possibilities extended to include the earth itself – Australia is a travel narrative. The desire or necessity to move on, has given and continues to give our world its shape (4).

According to Davidson taking a leaf from the Aborigine's inclusion of the earth itself reflected in their philosophy necessitate the possibility of travel writing to include the local by articulating the psychological and inner journey brought about by the act of being self-conscious. Rather that just accounting for the physical journey, travel journalism involves the capturing of the intricacies of the interior consciousness propelled by that desire to find meaning for ones existence. This explains why travel writers engage in self-referencing in accounting to their reader the movement from point a to point b.

Colin Thubron in an interview "Writers Talk" with Malise Ruthuen notes travel travel journalism is one civilization commenting on another. He further notes that the connection of fiction with travel journalism is that both enhances the belief that 'out there the world is different' and hence a search for something which is not there (Video). Travel journalism, as a narrative genre, banks on the imagination and creativity of the writer as traveller to communicate the familiar to his/her audience in a manner that illicit in the reader a desire to discover something new. Travelling as a hobby or activity is embedded in the desire to change. Consequently, the author, through the power of words, communicates this change that he/she has experienced.

Examining Theroux's works "The trans Karoo Express to Cape Town" and "Blue train Blues," we deduce that the author defines travel journalism as a form of encountering new people and engaging them so as to learn about what makes them who they are. He deliberately selects the characters of his narrative to truthfully reflect the dynamics playing out in the setting of his story. Theroux's two travel pieces under scrutiny, with South Africa as the setting, provide a window through which the reader, local or foreign, comes to grasps, in a rather subtle way, with the deep-seated political and social economic nuances that exists outside the text. This resonates well with Daniel Lehman's notion where the reader, writer and subject of the narrative are each implicated materially and historically by the words on the page (1997).

Fox's "Doubling the wintry capes" and "Zimbabwe's wild side," articulate the writer's quest for travel, for the former as a curiosity for an experience and for the latter as a quest to find answers to the issue of human selfishness and cruelty to other creatures. In this way Fox offers us an understanding as to what travel journalism is. From Fox's two writings, we infer that travel journalism is a subjective account that makes logical sense of an experience of moving from point A to point B. In Fox's works this movement is more physical than psychological. Surprisingly, Fox in "Zimbabwe's wild side" offers a new insight for another aspect of travel journalism; that it is a journey pursuing the cause for animal right and preservation of nature.

Fox's story is weaved with a thread that opens the reader to issues and universal concerns of anti-poaching. Fox's intent for travel as articulated in "Zimbabwe's wild side," originates from a journalistic desire for truth. What makes this piece travel writing is the fact that it gives an account of the writer's encounter with the after effects of a sinking economy.

How does travel journalism differ from other kinds of journalism and non-fiction?

Travel journalism is different from other forms of journalism because of its relatedness to fiction. Other works of journalism, like hard news and news features, strive for objectivity at the expense of subjectivity. Writers of other kinds of journalism avoid narrating in the first person pronoun 'I' by distancing themselves from the narrative through the third person pronoun; 'he/she' or 'it'. In other words, other works of journalism focus on events as the centre of the narrative propelling its development.

Hartsock in "Introduction" distinguishes travel journalism from other kind of journalism by citing Sims argument that unlike standard journalism, literary (travel) journalism demands immersion in complex, difficult subjects (2000). Hartsock expresses the difference between travel journalism and non-fiction well again when he offers Connery's defense of literary journalism. For Connery the application of the word 'journalism' to travel is preferred over 'non-fiction' because of two reasons; namely (a) the works assigned to this literary form are neither essays nor commentary, and (b) much of the content of the works comes from traditional means of news gathering or reporting (2000). Theroux is the dominating character of his travel story and he makes the reader see his subjects through his own eyes. Though he brings in a lot of characters, each fading away as the story build up, he as character stays with the story to the end. There is no account of an event where he is not present, unless it is an event he is told by the characters he encounters or when he offers the historical aspects.

Theroux's "Trans-Karoo Express to Cape town" has news value just like hard news and news features, but it is not the type of news that is raw and immediate to fit hard news. For instance, the issue of district six, Nadine's novel July's People being classified as 'too racist,' Swanepoel's analysis of the state from the Boer perspective, the novel act by the Biehls family to forgive the killers of their daughter Amy Biehl in Guguletu and giving a job to these killers, all these are news worthy stories. Therefore, the way Theroux blends these issues to the plot of his narrative distinguishes travel journalism from other forms of journalism.

Looking at Fox's "Zimbabwe's wild side" the difference between other kinds of journalism and travel journalism becomes more evident. Fox's piece brings out the problem of poaching in a more concrete and personalised way drawing the reader to feel with the experience. Fox's approach and style may appear accidental at the first instance, yet it embodies the journalistic values of search for verifiable truths. If Fox were to write a news piece on the discovery of the poachers in Chazarira National Park, he would have recorded the facts of the seizure and stoppage of the poachers. Lacking the subjective flair the piece would have been foreign and failed to bridge the distance between the reader and the subject of the narrative. But in the form of travel writing this story is alive to the reader and it has the potential of eliciting a positive response in him/her to this social injustice. Therefore, in this analysis we concluded that travel journalism, unlike other kinds of journalism, brings 'home' the story and makes the reader relate to what is contained on the page.

Both Fox and Theroux utilizes a technique that Lehman discusses as the indeterminacy of the text, a quality that travel journalism, non-fiction writing and other forms of journalism have in common. Travel journalism applies conventional generic markers similar to hard news stories and new features. Theroux and Fox develop their travel pieces in question by utilizing this technique profusely. The larger portion of "Doubling the wintry capes" develops in a narrative format that utilizes, through a logical connection, quotes from those travelling on the Safmarine with Fox. For example, the first four lines of the story are weaved by use of this technique. Similarly, Theroux applies the same techniques in his two stories. Hard news would only apply this technique to respond to the news pyramid structure without following a plot as travel journalism would.

Other forms of non-fiction writing such as essays, reports and journal articles differ, too, from travel journalism specifically in structure and style. Theroux and Fox, though, they utilize other texts such as reports and archive material in the same way other forms of non-fiction do, at least in their travel writing, these materials assume a narrative flow. The historical material (referential) used in the travel pieces by the two writers fits with the narrative rather than standing out as stale information. For instance, in Theroux's pieces, "Captain Cook and Charles Darwin and Scott of the Antarctic and Rudyard Kipling and Mark Twain and many others who had rounded the Cape had stopped in this beautiful harbour" (2002: 488).

The aim and specific preoccupation of travel journalism.

It is apparent that Theroux's travel pieces bring to the fore two distinct aims of travel that later on translates into a classical piece of travel journalism. Firstly, there is the justifiable desire to disconnect from the routinely happenings of ones life, a run-away from the familiar; distancing oneself from the immediacy of technology. Secondly, it is the desire to feed curiosity, finding out what has changed in the places visited. Theroux implicitly explains what travel means to him in the introduction "Lighting Out" in his book *Dark Star Safari: Overland from Cairo to Cape Town* (2002: 3). He confesses that;

> Out of touch in Africa was where I wanted to be. The wish to disappear sends many travellers away. If you are thoroughly sick of being kept waiting at home or at work, travel is perfect: let other people wait for a change. Travel is a sort of revenge for having been put on hold, or having to leave messages on answering machines, not knowing your party's extension, being kept waiting all your working life – the home bound writer's irritants. But also being kept waiting is the human condition (2002: 3).

It is this self-awareness that forces Theroux to travel and to some degree accords him the audacity and twist to weave the narrative from Cairo to Cape Town. We infer from Theroux's confession that travel journalism involves documenting the inner conflicts that leads one to the travel and how the act of travelling negotiates the deep seated need to find something better away; in other territories. 'Something better' in this sense implies what rests in the desire to be let free and remain undisturbed; the search for an inner space, rather than the aesthetical implication in terms of a physical space, that might be denoted by the term 'better.' It is the response to this inner conflict that travel provides which creates the twist through which Theroux develops his plot. As it where, travel journalism not only becomes an account of the physical movement; a transformation from point 'a' to point 'b,' but also a description of an inner psychological and imaginative (self-referencing) journey. In this case, Theroux accounts for how he finds that sense of peace and serenity in a land deprived of modern technological and communication innovations.

The preoccupations of travel journalism, identified in the pieces examined in this essay, are (i) an engagement with that which is other than the self and different from the familiar, (ii) seeing and judging other cultures and civilization from the vantage point of the writer who is a traveller at the same time, and also (iii) the unveiling of the inner consciousness as the self is subjected to that desire to be changed by what lays beyond. Above all, the preoccupation of travel journalism is primarily embedded in the term 'discovery.' The three numerated factors all strives for a discovery that is both "an inner and outer process" (13) for the traveller who is also writer. Therefore, it is these factors that form the fabric of Theroux and Fox's works.

Fox in "Zimbabwe's wild side" is engaged with the realities of an impoverished society that has no sense of preserving wild life. This is an engagement with the unfamiliar. Fox is fascinated with this reality because it creates that inner conflict with his worldview. All things being equal and they are not; this engagement gives the narrative life capable of capturing the reader's attention. This is also true of Theroux's piece "Trans-Karoo Express to Cape town" and "Blue train blues." Theroux, just like Fox, engages with different cultures still wrestling with the baggage of their history.

In the same piece Fox makes judgment on those he encounters from his worldview; which is rather informed. For instance, he articulates the supposedly inefficiency of the Zimbabwean police when he notes that "not having much faith in Zimbabwe's police force we feared they might be apathetic…maybe send one man with a rusty revolver" (2). Also, the communication of his concerns against anti poaching derives from his informed knowledge and worldview different from the poachers. For example, he argues "poaching, even if it's at subsistence level, destroys a resource which will be one of the few cash cows when Zimbabwe emerges from this dark phase" (3). This is surely, contrary to the worldview of the illegal poachers who struggle with issues of bread and butter by resorting to simple solutions germane to the Iron Age.

Fox is very much moved by that inner desire to be changed by what lays beyond. In this story the motive to travel was sparked by the stories of the illegal poachers taking advantage of the ill situation in their midst. This desire leads Fox to travel and make a discovery both inside and outside the self. The outside discovery is encountering the illegal poachers, hence confirming the stories told before. The motive behind this desire is anchored in the journalistic quest to find the truth. This inner discovery brings out the conflict with the plot, or a reverse in the unfolding of the plot. It is the realization of the humanness Fox share with the poor wounded poacher, as it where, feeling for him. He notes that, "I felt snared in complicity and urged the cops to get him to the clinic as soon as possible" (2).

Theroux's two pieces are so apparent in showing that he is meeting 'the other' as he keeps identifying his characters by their nationality, 'the Japanese,' 'Italian woman,' and the 'English couple.' These clarifications of people are justified though. Further still, he feels at liberty in making crude comments on those he describes. For instance, "in spite of his shaven head and missing teeth and bike-madness, Chris had a zen-like view of the world and he discouraged any belittling of the state of the world, Africa include" (466).

What makes a prose text qualify as travel journalism?

Connery's definition of literary journalism if applied to travel journalism would clarify what makes a prose text to qualify as travel journalism. Connery purports that this kind of journalism is "non-fiction printed prose whose verifiable content is shaped and transformed into a story or sketch by use of narrative and rhetorical techniques generally associated with fiction" (1997). Thus, travel journalism is prose that documents true happenings through the use of fiction techniques; qualifying the adage, 'facts in need of fiction.' Whereas, prose or fiction deals with the creative imagination of the writer to communicate truth-values travel journalism utilizes the same techniques to communicate news values from a body of true accounts and happenings. The only difference between travel journalism and fiction is that the latter is aimed at the transmission of moral teachings. Travel journalism as a true account of an experience is not aimed at offering a moral teaching.

Just as fiction uses figures of speech such as irony, metaphor, simile, paradox, euphemism, hyperbole, parable and many such styles to comment on everyday happenings, also travel journalism put to use these techniques as a way of reinforcing the imagery power of the narrative. For instance, the style and format of Fox's piece "Zimbabwe's wild side," reads as though it is a work of fiction yet it is an account of a true story applying fictional style. His use of figures of speech to create a picture of what was happening is so strong, for example, "No sooner had I arrived than an electric storm rolled in. We watched it coming from the magnificent pool-and-braai deck. Vanguard rainbows marched out front and an ethereal light bathed camp as we waited for the downpour," (1) "all hell broke loose"(2) and "European bee-eaters enjoyed in-flight meals of termites elates emerging from their mounds like dandelions against a low sun" (2). This technique he applies too in "Doubling the wintry capes." For instance, "Squeezing a skyscraper through the eye of the needle. The screws begin to turn, lathering our stern. The deck begins to pulse like the skin of a breathing leviathan" (1) and the phrase, "it peels away and describes a shape turn, back into the port's safety," (1) are powerful application of fiction style that liven the narrative. Equally, Theroux uses figures of speech in "The Trans-Karoo Express to Cape Town," such as "The house on the slopes of Devil's Peak was so buffeted by the powerful westerly that parked cars trembled on their tires and window panes distorted reflections like fun house mirrors because the glass was pressed and sucked by the gusts" (472) and many such. It is by the use of figures of speech that makes the narrative a work of prose. Consequently, this prose duels with actual happenings in the real world of matter and as such qualifying for travel journalism. Thubron cautions the writer of travel journalism that one should be fascinated by actuality than fictionalizing the account (Writers Talk, video).

David Velleman in his article "Narrative Explanation" poses a very cardinal question about "what makes a story specifically good as a story…is its excellence at organizing events into an intelligible whole" (2002: 3). This is what makes both Theroux and Fox's stories qualify as travel journalism. Theroux's brings together his experiences in exploring Africa and wanting to see if Africa had changed at all from forty years ago when he worked there as a teacher and the desire to be lost in Africa. Fox, moved by the quest to verify the reports of poaching in the national parks of Zimbabwe, arranges his narratives well the encounter with fellow travellers, the illegal poachers and the proprietor of the lodge. In the Safmarine story he manages, through application of the conversional generic markers, to hold together an account of his curiosity to travel on shore from Durban to Cape Town. In a way, both Theroux and Fox have utilized a mode that looks for a twist to create a fragmented narrative blend in perfectly well to satisfy the plot.

Using Lehman's words, what makes prose qualify as travel journalism, being a work of non-fiction, the writer produces a document for the audience that reads history as both text and experience, an audience that is engaged over the edge, by what exists both within and without the text (1997: 5). According to Lehman, travel journalism could be said to be a piece of work that is the site of both artistic and social engagement, an engagement that contexts the manner by which we apprehend and communicate experiences (1997: 42).

Further still, to paraphrase Lehman's conception of literal journalism, it can be argued that a prose qualifies to be travel journalism when it purports to re-enact for the reader the play of actual characters and events across time. As Lehman further puts it, these accounts phenomena are available to and experienced by the reader outside the written artifact.

Another major qualifier of a piece of prose to be termed travel journalism is when it makes use of both the referential (outside) and reflexive (inside) literal facilities of non-fiction. Both Fox and Theroux's stories applies these techniques perfectly. Fox applies the referential techniques when he notes in "Doubling the wintry capes," Yael Adams' age, background and the fact that she is destined to be the first coloured captain in the fleet (2). Theroux uses the reflexive facility in "Blue Train Blues" when he notes, "the train was almost heartbreaking for being so pleasant, for offering this view of South Africa, the same misery, the same splendour. But also my work was done, my safari ended. This trip was just a dying fall; I was clinging to Africa because I had not wanted it to end" (2002: 493). These two literally facilities; namely referential and reflexive are well summed up by Lehman when he explores the theory of non-fictional narrative as implicated text.

Lehman argues further that an "implicated reading becomes all the more valuable and troubling if we explore some distinctions between non-fiction and fiction at the level on which the narrative interacts with historical experience and if we examine for its practices and ideology" (1997: 7). According to

Lehman, the writer of fiction is free to maneuver whereas the writer of the non-fiction must abide by the conditions of his lease. Fox's uses the referential technique, for instance, in "Zimbabwe's wild side," when he notes that;

> Poaching, even if it's at subsistence level, destroys a resource, which will be one of the few cash cows when Zimbabwe emerges from this dark phase. To have white Zimbabweans from the private sector teaming up with parks board and regional police in anti-poaching initiatives has got to be good. Despite being Zanu-PF controlled – and contrary to much shrill reporting – parks and police are staffed with many concerned individuals wanting to preserve their national heritage (3).

Travel journalism has a thread; single or multiple, through which the plot develops and the author assumes a prominent role as a character in the narrative. In hard news and news features the writer's presences, as a character in the story is insignificant. Like some non-fiction, travel journalism identifies with journalistic works that ascribe to the maxim "facts in need of fiction."

The techniques of writing shown in the selected texts:

There are four major techniques used by both Theroux and Fox that I find helpful in constructing creative pieces of travel journalism. The four techniques are the use of figures of speech, referential, reflexive and dialogue format. In addition to these, I also find Theroux's sarcastic yet humorous treatment of his characters very helpful too. This essay has actually managed to show how both Theroux and Fox utilizes these techniques in their works. I will therefore, discuss how I have applied these techniques in my travel journalism piece entitled "Camping in Room 13." In this sense making a conclusion to the essay through this discussion of my work in relation to Theroux and Fox's travel writings.

The figures of speech I apply in the story for instance, "She looked spherical like a soccer ball" and "The warm sissy on the side snored like a lioness" (2006: 2). I also use a metaphor consistently to give an imagery of war in the application of words and phrases such as eruption, boom, siege, Hiroshima, Nagasaki. The other metaphor I apply symbolizes the image of hardness. I use phrases like 'the concrete jungle,' 'heart of stone,' 'I felt like a stone' and 'I slept like a log.' I also use an idiom "a square peg in the round hole."

In the story I apply the technique of referential by citing the historical background of Mafikeng. I note that;

> Here I was in Mafikeng, a town made world famous by a siege during the Anglo-Boer War of 1899. During the Siege of Mafikeng Colonel Robert Baden-Powell first used boys as "Scouts," taking messages and assisting in the town. The 217 days' town relief had raised Baden-Powell, in Britain, to the status of a hero. This earned fame and popularity had resulted in the founding of the Scout Movement a few years later. Mafikeng, now houses internationally renowned camping sites for scouting in the game reserves.

This technique, just like Fox and Theroux had applied it in their pieces, fits well with the subject of my travel narrative. This historical aspect resonates perfectly with the imagery of war that the figures of speech employed in the narrative. Also the name Mafikeng meaning a place of stone holds together with the simile in the story "I felt like a stone" and "the human heart is like a place of stones" and also calling the city 'the concrete jungle."

In the travel story "Camping in Room 13" the reflexive technique is sparingly applied. For instance, in this passage I use my imagination to reflect on the reality before me. Thus utilizing the reflexive facility I note that,

> There were no birds singing, dogs bucking or cats mewing. I could feel the weight and discomfort in my bladder. "Should I pee against the walls on the side of the shops?" I wondered. There was no bush in sight and other vehicles were passing one after another at what seemed like century intervals. I recalled my scouting days, with all its love of adventures; having to find ones' way out by a good eye capable of reading signs. Here I was in Mafikeng, which now for me was a semi-concrete jungle. I adopted that optimistic-scout maxim, 'always be prepared.'

The reflexive technique is a technique that allows the writer to be conscious of what is happening and constantly asking questions. Perhaps, this explains what Thubron articulates in the interview "Writers Talk" that there is a desire in the traveller to discover what is not there by imaging that there is something different out there.

In the travel piece I also utilize quotes that have internal monologues and external dialogues. For instance, I quote the voice of my imagination; "This isn't a nightmare," and "Should I pee against the walls on the side of the shops?" Further still, I apply the dialogue for example:

"Yes," I shouted in response, still uncertain of the intruder.

"Breakfast is at six in the dinning hall," called the voice behind the door.

"Ok, thank you," I said in a rather disarmed tone.

Quotes liven up the narrative by making it flow smoothly. There is no strain in the reader to understand what the writer is trying to communicate. However, it is a skill to know what type of quotes to include and which ones not to include. It is not all quotes that are relevant to the flow of the story just as not every action is significant to the narrative. Journalism is about selecting events so is travel journalism.

In my story the description of the man who enters the bus to occupy the seat beside "brother" is a technique of sarcastic humour. Welcoming the lady on the seat and later making remarks about her weight offers a contradiction in a humorous twist.

The most important and helpful lesson to be got from Fox and Theroux is the application of fiction techniques to the factual material in the hands of the travel writer. And just as Thubron notes in the interview the writer needs to be fascinated by the actual events embellish them through his/her imagination and creativity and not to fabricate events. The Mafikeng trip taught me to probe the imagination and make sense of what at first I thought would not make good reading as a work of travel journalism.

Questions for reflection:

1. How is travel journalism different from other kinds of journalism like sports and politics?
2. Is it ethical to apply techniques of fiction to travel journalism?
3. Is it easy to incorporate dialogue in a piece of travel journalism?
4. What is the advantage of using self-referencing and historical devices in constructing travelogues?

Chapter Nineteen
Assessment Narrative

I have always been fascinated by the idea of knowing who I really am. Over the years I have undergone several processes of self-evaluation and peer-evaluation in order to understand and know myself. I have reflected on my life on many occasions and also I have received several feedbacks from companions and superiors, especially in my religious life. In the past I have used the anagram and other instruments to understand myself. The process of self-discovery has been a daunting as well as exciting exercise for me. Most of these assessments I have taken before have been based on looking at what my strengths and weaknesses are and how I should improve in the future.

I took the Thomas-Kilmann Conflict Mode Instrument (TKI). This is the first assessment program that I took that helped me to understand myself fully. This assessment looks at the conflict-handling modes especially when trying to negotiate meeting one's own concerns (Assertiveness) in the process of attempting to meet those of another person's (*Cooperativeness*). I was surprised to find out that *avoiding* stood out the most used mode instead of *accommodating* which come out second. Both *accommodating* and *avoiding* ranked higher. *Collaboration* and *compromising* ranked moderate, which for me was not really satisfying. I would have expected *avoiding* to appear third after *accommodating* and *collaborating*. I usually *accommodate* others when I am in charge for instance, in a classroom situation. I also found out that I collaborate well with people who think like me and those who seem to have better ideas. *Avoiding* comes especially when there is an issue that would bring conflict and I do not agree with it. If there are strong characters I tend to withdraw and let the others ideas prevail. It was equally surprising to discover that *competing* was ranked last with no score at all. I am very poor in asserting myself but usually when I find there are people who are not assertive like me then I tend to come out of the shell and lead the way. So there are opportunities when I find myself running the show. When I am in charge of leading a task I find myself very assertive. But given the results in this assessment that competing is at the bottom, it implies that I lean more on the unassertive and cooperative modes. However, looking back at my own life I realize that I most of the time choose to avoid or withdraw when found in conflicting situations. During team-work tasks I have realized that I tend to withdraw and never assert myself especially when I am not in charge of the group. I have also found out that I am more *accommodating* to other people's opinions and options. The *introversion* aspect of energizing myself auger well with the concept of *avoiding* which lean more on drawing energy from within.

I had heard about the Myers-Briggs Type Indicator (MBTI) while teaching psychology to college students. It has four segments that help to explain one's personality, namely: *introversion* or *extroversion* (*how I energize myself*) (Katharine, C. Biggs & Isabel B. Myers, 1998), sensing or intuition (*how I gather information*)(Biggs, 1998), thinking or feeling (*how I make decisions*) (Biggs, 1998); and finally judging or perceiving (*how I interact with the world around me*) (Biggs, 1998). The results I got from the MBTI were the preferences of *introversion*, intuition, thinking and judging (INTJ). I am a person who draws strength from within hence I was not surprised with the clear score of *introversion* aspect. I tend to work well if I have time to myself. The results in how I gather information indicated intuition on a moderate level. I am a person who thinks much about the future. Also on making decisions I tend to think over things or rather figure out issues in a more logical way (*Thinking*). The results were moderate on this one too. Though I do lean more on using logic in decision-making, I have found myself balancing between thinking and feeling. On how I interact with the world around me the results showed that I am judging and this came out very strongly. I am a person who wants to have programs in place and everything set in time before I venture into it. My only surprise with this result is that it came out strongly. Anyhow, I see myself often wanting to know in advance what I am expected to do. I like to have things planned out and when I am found in a situation that things are not clear I tend to panic or rather I get confused.

The third assessment test I took was the Emotionally Intelligent Leadership (EILS: 1). This inventory assesses how one controls personal emotions especially when one is dealing with the self and others during teamwork.

The EILS: 1 Inventory has three-tier facets that contribute to the leadership dynamic, namely: consciousness of context; consciousness of self; and consciousness of others. After taking this assessment I discovered that my area of strength was in the consciousness of context. I am often aware of the work environment and situation. My surprise was to discover that the consciousness of the others appeared third though I would have expected it to appear second after consciousness of the self. I have always thought that I am very much aware of myself and others more than I am aware of context. However, the consoling factor is that the differences in the margin among these facets were minimal. With this I was satisfied to learn that actually I move freely across these facets. My area of strength is the facet of consciousness of the self with the capacity for empathy and emotional self-perception. These facets are the opposite of my MBTI facet of the thinking and the judging. However, my area of growth is the consciousness of others, conflict management, avoiding and teamwork. Though I enjoy collaborating and cooperating with others I have most of the time failed to be effective in group-work.

The last assessment I took was the Gallup Strengths Finder. This assessment gives the five top themes, which are explained, in three sections, namely; awareness, application, and achievement (Gallup, 2012). The top five themes results for me were connectedness, responsibility, learner, strategic and achiever. This assessment only indicates the strengths in the positive light. This is empowering because it helps one grow by looking at things that build rather than those that bring down. I see connectedness in the sense that I believe that everything happens for a reason. I am here where I am today due to the fact that my past experiences build me to this level. The facet of responsibility comes in the sense that I am most of the times loyal to people and that I take ownership of what I say. The learner facet shows up in my desire to learn and improve every time. The strategic facet is also present in me in the sense that I think over things before I do them. Also I am never challenged by failure as I always look up for other alternatives or ways of doing things. The achiever facet is shown in how I work hard in most of the responsibilities I have had in the past.

Performance Review

As a religious moving out a house of formation in 2011, I was expected to evaluate myself as regards my life of prayer, community life, apostolate and vowed life. The question I would ask myself is that: How have I grown in these areas? Then I would write a three-page paper and present it to the superior to go through after which we would meet. I did one of these assessments some three years ago. I found out that I was an *introvert* who enjoyed more time to the self and also working mostly by me. I discovered that I enjoyed company of others in as far as it came to work together for a common goal. I felt I was emotionally attached to my work of assisting the young homeless of Nairobi, Kenya. I would chat with them and help them find ways of improving and expanding their self-reliant project of running a garden and selling vegetables. In assisting these young boys I would *collaborate* well with other religious friends assigning them duties.

Peer Feedback

All the five respondents, who included friends and one youth I worked with, organized their feedback into strengths and weaknesses. Of the four friends, I was surprised to have assertiveness on the top. They also indicated that I was self-motivated and owned my actions and words. The facets that all the five emphasized was that I was focused and also was open to new ideas. One of the respondents who happen to be a pastoral psychologist highlighted the idea that my self-esteem was admirable. What is impressive with this observation is that though I sometimes appear laid-back I have self-confidence especially that I am an *introverted* person. These augur well with my MBTI configuration of INTJ. This implies that I am an original thinker and I have a great drive to implement and achieve my goals. It agrees with the Gallup Strength Finder facet of leaner.

One of the weaknesses that come out in two of the respondents was that I was too reserved and lacked the charisma to attract friends and make relationships. Another weakness mentioned by all the four was that they were not sure on how I handle conflict situations. This corresponds with the Thomas-Kilmann Conflict Mode Instrument, which offers me a result of withdrawal as high and also competing as low. Given this feedback, it can be concluded that my areas of growth are the ability to make friends, assert myself, and manage conflicts.

Conclusion

These assessments discussed above fit-in well with what I am and what I am to become. The reserved personality, focused, non-conflict taker and a healthy self-esteem explain well the person I am. One of the feedbacks indicated an element of *accommodating* other people's ideas just like the TKCMI had indicated. All in all, these assessments are supposed to assist me better comprehend myself, others and the world around me. Nonetheless, these are not cast-in-concrete facets as there is always an opportunity for moving from one facet to the other. For instance, the element of assertiveness which did not appear in most of the assessments yet appeared in the feedback. These shifts would always, in a sense, provide room for improvement and growth.

Chapter Twenty

Communication and Human Understanding

Francis Bacon (1605), book, *The Advancement of Learning* offers insights on what we could call his theory of communication based on scientific method of inquiry, which utilizes an empirical and inductive approach. Bacon equates inquiry for knowledge with the search for truth. He argues that knowledge is discovered by observation and experience and that empirical knowledge is rooted in the natural world. For him true knowledge is in the contemplation of nature and observation of experience. In his evaluation of human learning he notes two barriers to knowledge or truth; namely that: (i) man sought truth in their own little worlds, and not in the great and common world, and that (ii) man had an impatient of doubt and haste to assertion without due and mature suspension of judgment. Bacon's assertion is that, "If a man begins with certainties he shall end in doubts, but if he be content to begin with doubt he shall end with certainties" (Hughes, Glyn, 2011. For Bacon, knowledge takes away barbarism, vain admiration of anything, which is the root of all weakness. It invests and crowns man's nature, premeditation and invention.

Bacon identifies three parts of human understanding applied in the arts as history, poesy and philosophy, which he notes, appeal to man's memory, imagination and reason. In communication this would entail utilizing narratives or stories that one can relate to, using effective sentences or language or images that capture the imagination, and disseminating a message that is convincing and logical. This triangulation method of appealing to memory, imagination and reason can be used to evaluate the generation of media content or text in the media, public relations and marketing.

In some societies the media wield a lot of power yet today media owners polarize the media due to vested interest. In the quest for human knowledge and the search for truth can the media be trusted? In developing countries and the developed world people look up to the media for help in finding answers to their questions on a number of issues; for instance, during election time which party do they need to vote for. Many media outlets because of polarization have each disseminated information to influence people's opinions and choices. The problem is that the media have tended to give people ready-made answers instead of allowing them to make up their mind by the facts presented. To discuss this problem, this paper will focus on news stories on television and how they are presented. To do this the paper will analyze a couple of television channels in both Kenya and Zambia. Then Bacon's theory of human understanding will be applied to show how the media can reclaim its power through communicating messages and images that assist people to come to the truth by appealing to memory, imagination and reason.

In Zambia, the public broadcaster Zambia National Broadcasting Co-operation (ZNBC) has always been used as a propaganda tool for any reigning political party. During the main news at 7 pm the first item would always focus on the republican president and also other political parties would never be given positive coverage. The news would involve newscasters parroting press releases from government officials over events attended by these same officials and the speeches given. Most of the time the newscasters would never give any analysis of the issues articulated by the covered government official or the republican president. The news would always be a presentation of biased facts.

During the 2011 presidential campaign this model of news bias covering only the ruling party failed to be effective. Many people would not watch news on the public broadcaster because they believed that the news did not reflect the reality of Zambian politics. Despite the republican president having enjoyed full coverage he ended up losing the election to the opposition leader who had always been given negative coverage by ZNBC. In this sense ZNBC was no longer credible in helping the viewers discover the truth from the media. The media failed to utilize Bacon's model of discovering the truth through observation and experience in the natural world. ZNBC's news model is a reflection of most public broadcasters in the world. However, though most private broadcasters can be also biased due to vested market interest, there are a few that provide an alternative from the propaganda model of most public broadcaster world over.

In Kenya, one of the private television channels, Kenya Television Network (KTN) has a model in its news broadcast that is effective due to its in-depth analysis of issues and hard line stance that provide check and balances on governance, instead of the mere reporting of news. For instance, during the period of the constitutional making process there were many contentious issues as regards particular clauses to be included in the new constitution. Unlike the national public broadcaster, Kenya Broadcasting Co-operation (KBC) that just reported raw news KTN had news reporters analyze the clauses offering insight on the bone of contention. KTN's aggressive approach, which was issue, based relied on qualified journalists who had done their research and subjected issues to rigorous analysis. In this way it helped the viewers understand issues reported thereby enabling each of them make an informed decision in the referendum that followed. KTN would do the same also during the presidential and parliamentary campaign periods. It would give equal coverage to all contestants in the election and analyze each candidate based on his/her stance on pertinent issues such as health, education, land and the like.

KTN news in its analysis and narration of issues presented facts in a model that takes its viewers from the known to the unknown hence tapping from what people already know from the past. Basically, what most viewers would know would either be unverified roomers or ear say and KTN would feed them with the missing information. Hence, like Bacon's assumption, some viewers who would have thought they knew everything would be led to realize that they were missing the truth and those who had doubts would be led to the discovery of the truth.

Further still, KTN's news was based on observation and the experience of the Kenyan society. In its news presentation it would utilize words and images would evoke people's imagination. For instance, on the issue of either to include the abortion clause in the constitution, KTN had medical practitioners from either side of the debate. It also made use of opinions from a sample of the Kenyan population. In this sense, the news analysis in its presentation and arguments challenged people's reasoning and helped them appreciate the truth. Therefore, KTN's model applied well Bacon's theory of truth searching through observation and experiences in the real world unlike KBC and ZNBC.

Bacon's theory of scientific inquiry can be applied to journalism, public relations and marketing as an effective way of communicating the truth. Apparently, objectivity in journalism, public relation and marketing calls for the communicator to take a step aside from oneself and look at an issue in a more critical way. A good example is that of the CNN's international business correspondent Richard Quest, presenter of the program called "Quest means Business." In one of his series last September he hosted politicians from the European Union. In asking about the economy he played the devil's advocate, stepping aside and asking critical questions which he confessed at the end of the program as not reflecting his personal views but a way of seeking clarification for those who think differently.

In some parts of the world journalists, public relations officers and those in marketing lack the critical approach and in-depth analysis of issues and messages when they communicate their message. In marketing telling stories or narratives about the product is an effective way of persuading and retaining customers. These communicators in order to be effective they must also apply the styles of fiction like metaphors, similes, hyperbole and other figures of speech. In addition they must also present their material in a systematic, logical and critical way.

Media consumers are not *tabula rasa* that should be presented with only information and unsubstantiated facts. Information and facts must be presented in a way that gives credibility and legitimacy to the communicator because of the background work invested in the process of generating media content or text. Objectivity and truth telling in presenting media content entails that the communicator of any media text realizes that the consumer of the media text brings in his/her own subjectivity to the media text before him/her. It is the duty of the communicator to facilitate this interaction between the media content consumer and the media text before him/her. Media content generation should be subjected to a rigorous scientific inquiry based on the empirical and inductive approach. Both observation and human experience are related to the empirical and inductive approach of scientific inquiry.

In conclusion, this paper has shown how Bacon's theory of scientific inquiry is and can be effective in communication. Bacon's triangulation model of appealing to memory, imagination and reason is efficacies in the generation of media content and text as well as in evaluation of the media content and text. Future media researchers to analyze new media and social media content and text can apply this model.

Chapter Twenty One
Media messages

Communication theorists from Aristotle to contemporary scholars have been interested with the idea of audiences and how these consume the media messages and images. The theorists have attempted to indicate some form of clear-cut structures showing how the audiences are affected by what they consume in the media. Communication has been evolving in an unprecedented way just like Marshal McLuhan had put it in his idea of the 'global village.' The way Aristotle, the middle ages, modern and contemporary communicators approached communication was certainly different form one epoch to the other. Hence, the concept and reality of the audience during different epochs was relatively different.

Given the differences in the perception of what an audience would be in the stages of communication evolution, this essay, through triangulation, will analyze theories of Aristotle (George Kennedy, 1994), Kenneth Burke (1969) and Stuart Hall (1980) in order to come up with a communication theory and concept of audience that would fit the contemporary communication platform of social media, specifically Facebook. The paper will first compare and contrast the three communication theories of Aristotle, Burke and Hall and thereafter identify a new theory that would be used to explain the contemporary form of communication and audience as brought about by the emergence of the social media, specifically Facebook as a media platform.

Aristotle's (Kennedy, 1994) canons of rhetoric namely invention, arrangement, style, memory and delivery over the years have helped communicators package and present their massage or speech in a more professional way. Each of these five stages is very cardinal and a means to the end, which is communication. The five stages stretches from the period of planning, writing and executing the speech. Somehow this process requires that one is meticulous with details to make the speech hold together in a more coherent and realistic way that should capture not only the attention of the listener but also his or her imagination as well. What is cardinal here is that deliberate preparation is very important in communication. The focus of each of the five stages is and has been very important especially in safeguarding the effectiveness of the speech on the listeners/audience.

Usually at the invention stage is where the communicator does research and discovers arguments and then does pre-writing. At the arrangement stage the communicator organizes his/her arguments in a way that would make him/her achieve the aim of communication. At the style stage the communicator makes choices on the type of words, sentences, imagery and metaphors or other figures of speech is going to use and how these will be relevant to both the message and the listeners/audience. At the memory stage the communicator applies several mnemonic devices to assist him/her recall the parts of the oration. This is what educators would call the application of rote-memory to retain the subject to be taught. At the final stage which is delivery most for the speech the communicator works on oral presentation. These five canons work very well with speech preparation, writing and delivery. The question to be asked, especially with the contemporary communication challenges, is that can this approach work for social media like Facebook? This is the focus of this paper to see how these canons can be utilized in collaboration with others to come up with a more effective communication approach that emphasizes on planning, documenting and presentation or delivery.

For Aristotle (Kennedy, 1994) these five canons are anchored on his three basic principles of speech writing, namely *ethos*, *logos* and *pathos*. These three principles are very cardinal in terms of the message and the relationship with the audience. For instance, *ethos* denotes strategies one uses to convince the audience and also how credible the speaker is as regards the perception of the audience. *Logos* is about the text and the message to be communicated whereas *pathos* is on how the communicator appeals to the emotions of the audience through the way he/she presents the message. How do we apply these principles to social media like Facebook? This is the question that this paper will also strive to explain and discuss.

We can also look at Burke's (1969) theory of communication and see how it applied to communication and there after compare and contrast it with Aristotle's and see what could come out as a theory for social media.

Burke propounds the idea of identification and isolation professing that communication is an extension of our bodies. Human beings feel isolated from birth and that they have this desire to identify themselves with others. Therefore, language is one way that they manage to be identified. This theory of communication is human or individual centered. The communicator becomes the end of the purpose of the communication. The communicator is at one time the sender of the message but as he/she receives the feedback it makes him/her fulfilled because that feeling of isolation is replaced by identification. Burke's theory of communication meets the end of communication that is embedded in emotions. In this process of communicating the communicator, the message and the emotion appeal that the message brings between the communicator and the listener/audience are paramount to the aim and purpose of communication. Burke highlights language as the mode of communication but this language is not restricted to the spoken only as it can as well be written like in a speech or in other forms of medium like literature and music. How does this apply to social media like Facebook?

Stuart Hall (1980), in discussing encoding and decoding he replaces the passive and undifferentiated conception of the audience and replaced this with a more active conception of the 'audience.' He shows the relation between how media messages were encoded, the 'moment' of the encoded text and the variation of audience decoding. Unlike the traditionally conceptualized process of communication that was linear, Hall suggests a complex structure of relations that are distinctive moments, namely production, circulation, distribution/consumption, and reproduction. He argues that reality exists outside language, but it is constantly mediated by and through language. He stresses further that what we can know and say has to be produced in and through discourse. Thus there is no intelligible discourse without the operation of a code. Hall's theory of encoding and decoding was based on his analysis of film and television messages and images. How can this theory be applied to social media like Facebook?

An examination and analysis of the concepts of Aristotle, Burke and Hall could help us come to an understanding of how the blending of these three could be ideal for a theory of communication on social media, especially Facebook. The emphasis shall be put on the identification of the social media audience and how this new theory addresses their consumption of the media messages. For Aristotle we have inventory, arrangement, style, memory and delivery as the five canons. Then we also add his principles of *logos*, *ethos* and *pathos*. For Burkes we have isolation, association, and language. And for Hall we have production, circulation, distribution/consumption, and reproduction. These take place in the process of encoding and decode. We have also language that leads to discourse. Perhaps discussing each of these and see how they are related would help in formulating a theory for social media and the concept of audience in social media.

Blending these theories from Aristotle, Burke and Hall would of cause lead us to a new theory of social media. Encoding, production, circulation, logos, inventory, arrangement and style are related and they are at the preparatory stage of the media message. What is common here is the use of language and its packaging. The choice of words here is very important and also the way the arguments will flow also matters. This is one thing that we can find helpful also for the social media. Language carries with it that element of being able to persuade or create a response in the receiver/listener or audience. Decoding, *ethos*, *pathos*, memory, delivery, distribution/consumption, and reproduction are more linked with the presentation of the message by the communicator and the way it is received or interpreted by the recipient/audience. These theories present a more regulated form of communication. They are all presented as canons to be followed in order to communicate effectively and have an impact on the audience.

There are elements for each of the three theories that can work well with social media and they are those that cannot work well. These theories represent most the traditional form of communication like speech writing and delivery, interpersonal communication, and television production and programming. This implies that there is a lot of time taken in the preparation to the time of delivery. This might appear as a negative in relation to the Internet and Facebook that is instantaneous. However, Facebook might appear to be instantaneous but it does accommodate decoded messages that require time to produce. For instance, online publications that are a replica of traditional publication and also television and video streaming can be shared on Facebook. What is instantaneous is the chat room that does not allow the communicator to think through what he is communicating and also online publications that do not require verification because mostly they are products of citizen journalism. Therefore, the principles of encoding, decoding and language/discourse as propounded by Hall have a place in the social media. People place well thought out material on Facebook and people respond by liking, unliking, sharing, or by placing a comment. In terms of video streaming encoding and decoding takes place on the Facebook through Facebook users. Posting messages is a form of encoding. What is different with the traditional forms of communication to social media or Facebook is the fact that the later requires preparation of messages by choice of words and language while the former does not require rules for the language and choice of words. Whereas traditional forms of communication called for proper spellings and correct grammar social media has seen an abuse in this area. This abuse in some sense can be seen as a new development of shorthand and language for social media.

When we look at Aristotle's principles of logos, ethos and pathos we see that if we were to relate it to Facebook the ideas of logos and ethos would give us problems. There is little respect given to diction and grammar as discussed earlier for Facebook because the platform seems to promote its own language and word formulation. It negates the principle of proper spellings as its aim to communication and not the correctness of words or language. Therefore, logos does not have its place in social media.

As for ethos, the credibility of the person on Facebook is very questionable. Firstly, people mostly take on false identities on Facebook and it is very difficult to determine whether what people say or show on Facebook is a true reflection of themselves. Sometimes people create Facebook addresses of distinguished and high profile personalities trying to deceive people that they are a person who they are not. For instance, people sign in Facebook pages with the name of Mandela while it is someone else managing that account. Also people tend to communicate things they cannot say in an interpersonal relationship. People can carry out a character on Facebook that is totally opposite of themselves. Some communication scholars argue that:

> Credibility has been a long-standing issue in mass communication research. Even more than traditional media, the Internet raises issues of the accuracy, reliability, and adequacy of information. Chat rooms and multiplayer games raise questions of whether people are who they appear to be (Werner J. Se and James W. T, 2001:378).

This is very true of most of the accounts on Facebook but also there are people who are genuine. It is not everything that is on Facebook that is suspicious, for instance, some people like sharing relevant information they find on the Internet with their friends on Facebook. For instance, most of the news on Mandela's life was shared by people who had either read an online news portal with the news of Mandela or had watched a streamed video of president Obama's speech at the memorial of Mandela. So there are many resourceful material that people can share from the Internet through Facebook or any other social media. To support this argument, Severin and Tamkard further argue that people actually tend to rate Web publications as more credible than their traditional equivalents (379). This also concurs with Hall's five canons of communication.

These canons, namely production, circulation, distribution/consumption, and reproduction do work well on Facebook. Production is fast and easy either by generating self-content or by sharing what exists elsewhere on the Internet as reproduction. Then circulation, distribution/consumption cannot be separated from both production and reproduction because it is also instantaneous. One authority the communicator has on Facebook is to choose who the consumer of his media product would be and this audience is an active one. Social media provides immediate feedback on the message communicated and in a sense makes the producer and the consumer blend in as one. In the traditional communication scenario you would have a speechwriter or speaker and you'll have targeted audience but on Facebook these roles are blared and you have the producer who is at the sometime consumer of other media products on the platform.

When we consider *pathos*, consumption, emotions, delivery, isolation and association having this image in mind that on social media the producer and the consumer roles are interchangeably then we can easily imagine of a social media audience. On Facebook though there might not be that face-to-face interaction the emotions of both the producer and the consumer are evoked. Some people feel isolated as they cannot relate or socialize with the real world yet the expression the send or receive on Facebook make them addicted to the social network. So Facebook responds well to Burke's ideals of isolation and association and in that sense this canon of communication works well on this platform. People have been known to find life partners in marriage through social media. Because people are so busy with work, school or business those who cannot socialize in the real world have found a new language on the social media and their lives have changed.

Facebook as a social media has its merits and demerits it terms of forming human relationships and interaction. People have lost their resources because they trusted someone on social media but also people have managed to find their friends of ages or their partners on the same medium. There is an allowance for quick information on Facebook but also for well prepared and packaged messages too. So just like traditional forms of communication had their own defaults and positive attributes so does Facebook and other social media.

From the discussion in this essay it is actually possible to come up with a theory of communication for social media. This theory should embody elements like emotional appeal, credibility, and active audience. Facebook is not only a chatroom but it is a platform that even well planned and thought out messages are posted. Encoding on Facebook can be regulated just as exemplified in Facebook constant refusal to allow violence videos or pictures on it. Therefore, even if it is instantaneous there is possibility and room for regulating content and also to constantly check on accounts that are suspicious and have them deleted as it is done with online blogs and other social media. The consumers of Facebook actually have a mandate to report any messages that are violent or explicit in nature. With the development of new facilities on Facebook like 'share' and 'like' or 'unlike' the consumer has a say on what they read or watch on this platform. Therefore, the theory that this essay proposes for social media is that despite the flexibility of the language and choice of words Facebook needs regulation and monitoring. The question of audience on Facebook is also voluntary just as it is for traditional communication models.

The theory of communication for the social media or Facebook should be a circular one rather than a linear one and could look like this; sender/consumer/audience, encoding, decoding and feedback. Here it is to be understood that the sender who can also be a consumer is embedded with emotions that are present throughout the process of communication from the sender to the consumer, from encoding to decoding. This emotional edge is propelled by the fear of isolation and desire for identification. Encoding encapsulates all the need for preparation and the choice of language and diction that might be different from the traditional one. Decoding embraces the need for interpretation and personalization of the message communicated. This can be like contextualizing the message and getting the meaning that relates to the audience.

This new theory of communication for social media is an appreciation of Aristotle, Burke, and Hall's theories and a confirmation that social media can still fall within the strict regulation and canons of the traditional media. What the new platform, in case of Facebook, has done is to return the freedom to the audience to have a choice and a say in what he/she consumes and thereby provide immediate feedback. Facebook has blended the roles of producer and consumer/audience.

This essay has managed to discuss some of the theories of communication from the classic through the modern, the post-modern and the contemporary. It has argued that social media fits in the canons of these epochs and that from the past we can actually draw guidance to formulate a new and vibrant theory of communication for social media and also define what is meant by audience in the contemporary communication especially the age of social media.

Questions for reflection:

1. Is it true that social networking cannot be ethical because they are instantaneous?
2. Can we regulate social networks like facebook, tweeter and WhatsApp?

Chapter Twenty-Two

Zambia's Democracy and Development: Two Key Moments

In this essay I intend to address the issues of democracy and development in Africa, specifically looking at the case of Zambia. I shall give a general overview of Africa in a summary, a little background of Zambia's political and development history before the dawn of democracy (27 years of the founding father; President Kenneth Kaunda's reign), and finally I shall give an account of Zambia's experience of multi-party democracy vis-à-vis development during the ten years of President Frederick Chiluba's reign. The period of the reign of these former presidents spurns from 1964 to 2001. I shall discuss development in the sense of politics, infrastructure, economics and social service. Bearing in mind the religious and ideological inclination of Zambia, I will bring out how these aforementioned areas influenced development; especially that of the human person.

Democracy and Development

The Random House College Dictionary defines democracy as a "Government in which the supreme power is vested in the people and exercised by them directly or indirectly through a system of representatives usually involving periodical free elections." Schmitter and Karl in *Journal of Democracy* give an appropriate definition of democracy; they say that in, "modern politics democracy is the system of government in which rulers are held accountable for their actions in the public realms by citizens, acting indirectly through the competition and cooperation of their elected representative." Democracy in short is a government with the consent of the governed in which group relations are governed by rules of competition, compromise, and give-and-take.

In a democracy freedom is a by-product of a constitutional system of checks and balances, open and competing parties. Democracy gives power to the people and allows them to participate in the affairs of the nation. Leaders are primarily elected as representatives who have a mandate from the people to speak for them and bring forth development. A democratic environment favours competition, compromise and cooperation among the political parties. It is not only political parties that participate in safe guarding democracy but also institutions, organizations, societies and political parties.

Development is a broad term to define; mostly if related with a country and its politics. In this sense development is better analyzed through the wealth of a nation, its physical infrastructures, its governing and political systems and the well being of its people. A nation is developed if its political, social, economic and public systems address issues that affect its society and cooperate to address them for the common good of all. It would be important later on to link the idea of development with (Kenneth Kaunda's UNIP) Zambian Humanism and (Frederic Chiluba's MMD) the declaration of Zambia as a Christian Nation. According to Guy Arnold, "development is not separated from democracy, donors would maintain, but intertwined with it, at least if we accept in principle that development is about the welfare and advancement of the mass of the people." The Church defines development in terms of the human person. According to John Paul II development is a question of people. He argues that, "people are the subject of true development, and the aim of true development is people. The integral development of people is the goal and measure of all development projects."

Background

Zambia, then known as Northern Rhodesia, was a colony of British South African (B.S.A) Company from 1889 and Britain from 1924. The colonial rulers were interested in the exploitation of natural resources and human resources. The B.S.A. Company was interested in the mining of copper for export to the industrialized countries of the north. They colonial masters did not invest in any other economic activities but relied on the mining of copper.

The country had many untapped natural resources and potential land for agriculture that was underutilized. After independence, during the first republic, the United National Independence Party (UNIP) Government inherited an economy that was totally dependent on copper. At the time copy was rating well on the international market earning the country enough foreign exchange. The copper revenues provided for the national public investments. The government was able to provide services such as education, health, communication and many others. Apparently, development was at its best because it was during this period that most infrastructures, hospitals, schools and the two government universities in the country were built.

Twenty-Seven Years of Kaunda's (UNIP) Reign: Zambian Humanism.

Zambia got its independence from Britain on 24th October 1964. Kenneth Kaunda became its first president. He developed a philosophy of Zambian Humanism to guide and drive the Zambian dream. Humanism was approved as a Zambian ideology on 27th April 1967 by the UNIP National Council at a meeting in Matero; Lusaka. Clive Dillon-Malone in his book, *Zambian Humanism, Religion and Social Morality*, explains humanism well. He notes that the basic tenets of humanism can be found in many systems of thoughts; religious or non-religious. They are very much the core of the Christian gospel and universal human values. Zambian humanism has its central focus as the human person. It believes that human beings are basically and essentially good and that they are created in the image of God. However, due to the animal in man there is need for legitimate authority to protect and promote human rights of every individual. Malone notes that, Zambian Humanism, as a political ideology, is non-aligned, conciliatory, peace-oriented and cooperative. Zambian humanism reaches out to all in the spirit of friendship because its scope is universal or cosmic. It focuses on oneness of humanity and the need for the interdependence in all aspects of human relationships. It is against all forms of self-centered individualism. The state considers itself to be entrusted with the task of removing from society all exploitative and anti-social forces:

> We fight to eliminate all forms of evil. These include the philosophy of capitalism and its offshoots of imperialism, colonialism, neo-colonialism, fascism and racism in all their manifestations. Indeed we fight to eliminate anti-social forms of behavior such as greed, envy, oppression, self-indulgence, laziness, theft, plunder and murder, etc. all of which are exploitation of one man by another.

The two enemies of the humanist society are identified as capitalism as a socio-economic system and totalitarianism as a socio-political system. Zambian humanism fights exploitative capitalism with African socialism and totalitarianism with African participatory democracy. The model of African socialism is that of the extended family in which a communitarian relationship of individuals to one another is lived in practice. Though individuals have unique value and worth in themselves but their fulfillment can be understood in terms of their altruistic relationship with others in the wider society. Malone purports that, "the family relationship of respect for each other and every individual which finds meaning and fulfillment in relation to the whole family is the model on which social morality rests." Egoistic individualism is foreign to this communitarian model of African socialism. In Zambian Humanism, the family dimension of African socialism has found its universal expression in the social morality of the world religions and more specifically in the social teaching of Christianity. God is the universal Father and Christ is the universal brother to all men and women. As members of the one human family, all are expected to do to others, as they would have others do unto them. According to Kaunda the kind of socialism that Zambian humanism espouses is African democratic socialism. The focus is upon common ownership of national resources, which should not be confused, with State ownership. The main goal of African democratic socialism is to do away with all forms of exploitation but more especially those that are perceived to be intrinsic to the capitalist socio-economic system, which is identified with class oppression and greed. Hence, humanism tries to create an egalitarian society; a society in which there is equal opportunity for self-development for all.

The capitalist socio-economic system is considered to be dehumanizing both in its very nature and its effects. Zambian Humanism does not necessarily reject all aspects of capitalistic economic system, but rather what it refers to as 'unbridled capitalism.' It clearly recognizes the problem of the 'have' and the 'have nots' which expresses itself in various forms throughout history. These are all expressions of the sin or what Kaunda calls 'the animal in man' or sin in human societies. Furthermore, the movement towards perfection throughout history is not attributed to class struggle but to love. The revolutionary development identified in Zambian humanism is one of ever-growing unity into higher and more inclusive social forms in the movement from the family through tribe and nation to the universal society of love.

UNIP and its government established parastratal companies such as the Zambia Industrial and Mining Co-corporation (Zimco) (and many others). UNIP's prime program was to unite the nation by nationalization in all major institutions. It intended to shift the control of the economy from the hands of foreigners to the indigenous nationals. Humanism was the philosophy that was to drive national development because it was focused on "man" (person) as the centre of development. The UNIP government later on realized the impossibility of economic boost through this system of nationalization; it opted for 51% of shares in all major companies.

At about the mid 1980s copper prices at the international market deteriorated tremendously forcing the country's economy to fold. Unfortunately UNIP's policies on agriculture were not favorable to this industry. The government, like the colonial regime, did not invest in other sectors of the economy apart from copper mining. As a result the country had no alternative to boost its revenue than to turn to the donor communities. The greatest mistake Kaunda and the UNIP government made to the economy of Zambia could be best understood in the following factors: (i) The government controlled the major sectors of the economy such as mining, transport, agriculture, industry and many others by appointing managers to head them. Selection was not done on merit other than loyalty to the party. (ii) The government over-employed and under-paid its work force such that people were less kin to work for production. Hence, the government-run enterprises produced less and siphoned more of the tax payers' revenues for its existence. (iii) The general public treated government property with substantial abuse. (iv) Proper accountability and responsibility lacked in both the government and the Zambian population.

Despite the fledging economy Kaunda tried to maintain his role as a father of the nation by providing subsidies on health, education and essential commodities. Families used to receive coupons to collect millea-meal. This was done under the guise of the ideology of humanism, which only made the Zambian people lazy to fend for themselves.

The implementation of the philosophy of humanism was problematic given the economic challenges the country was facing. Zambian Humanism was good as it appeared on paper and its values were too idealistic. In practice it was difficult to maintain parastatal companies and to continue subsidizing education, health and social commodities. In the economic strata the lower sector was expanding and the government was running out of resources to sustain the parastatal companies. Zambian Humanism was not realistic given the Zambian economic situation at the time. Therefore, after 27 years of rule UNIP, Zambian Humanism and Kaunda became synonymous with failure, hence Zambia was a failed state.

Wind of Change across Africa

In the late 1980s and early 1990s the aura of democratization was sweeping across Africa replacing authoritative regimes. It was felt that for Africa to develop it had to change its political orientation and adopt a system that would promote a democratic environment which was envisaged as the ideal for development. For instance, the World Bank noted that, "Africa's future development will depend upon four major cornerstones: investing in people, sustaining adjustment efforts, improving the quality of governance and government institutions, and maintaining the momentum of donor assistance." The economic face in many African countries was tented with poverty, low foreign income capital, and high rates of inflation, unemployment, dilapidated infrastructures and myriads of other ills. Africa's economy became solely dependent on the international donor communities such as the World Bank (WB) and the International Monetary Fund (IMF). Firstly, the donor communities eluded the crippling economies of Africa to poor governance, lack of accountability and government intervention in the economy. The call for good governance and accountability from the Western countries and the donor communities forced African countries to adopt democracy as a form of government. Ake notes that the primary requirement for Africa's economic recovery in order to attain successful development is accountability, participation, and consensus building.

Multi-partism was regarded as the only sustainable alternative for Africa to develop. In fact multi-party democracy was presumed to be synonymous with development. Of course the process of democratization and the transition from single politics to multi-party politics were not easy for some countries in Africa. For instance, even at present, countries such as the Sudan, Zimbabwe, Morocco and Swaziland the process is still far from being realized. However, some countries like Zambia, Malawi, Tanzania and Ghana were fortunate to have a peaceful transition.

Most African countries became frustrated with the authoritative regimes, which liberated them from the colonial masters, particularly because they had raped national resources for self-aggrandizement. Most of these despots were not committed to development but were kin on uplifting their own glory. They drove the African economy to a sorry state while they bought themselves exorbitant cars and mansions.

Ten Years of Chiluba's (MMD) Reign: Declaration of Zambia as a Christian Nation.

Zambia was ruled by a single-party for 27 years when it returned to multi-party democracy in 1991. The first republic was under a multi-party system from independence in 1964 to 1972. The second republic was under one party state from 1972 to 1991. The third republic began in 1991 when the country returned to a multi-party system. During the presidential and parliamentary election on October 31 of 1991 the Movement for Multi-party Democracy (MMD) scooped 125 seats out of 150 seats. Multi-party representative democracy was opted in Zambia because people were desperate; they needed a change from the Kaunda's regime of one party participatory democracy.

During the last days of Kaunda's reign the economy was deteriorating. At the time Kaunda was associating himself with the Eastern religions; for instance, Hindu versions of the Marahishi Heaven on Earth project and the David Temple. Kaunda had allocated a huge amount of farmland to the Marahishi Heaven on Earth in the belief that they would be planting grass to be used for manufacturing fuel. The David Temple was a Hindu chapel that Kaunda was associated with though he was a professed Christian. Sichone and Chikulo note that:

> Part of MMD propaganda campaign against Kaunda was directed at his Indian spiritual advisor, Ranganathan. Vilified as a Guru who practiced all sorts of black magic, Ranganathan's name was used by MMD ideologues to 'prove' that Kaunda was not a Christian and on that basis state that the born again Chiluba was Zambia's first Christian president. To justify and validate this claim, Chiluba made a covenant with God soon after assuming office in November 1991 and declared Zambia a Christian state.

In the late 1960s Israel started constructing the University of Zambia (UNZA). In 1967 when Israel occupied the Gaza, Kaunda broke alliance with Israel on the basis of Israel instigating violence on the innocent. Kaunda stopped the Israel government from continuing to construct the university after they had done about 20% of the construction.

Due to Kaunda's association with Eastern religions and his bleach of contract with Israel, Chiluba accused Kaunda's regime of apostasy and anti-Semitism. Chiluba had become a born again Pentecostal while in prison under treason charges. Chiluba associated himself with American tele-evangelists like Benny Hinn and Ernest Angely. These American evangelicals are associated with neo-liberalism. They worship the God of prosperity. According to Chiluba, the Kaunda regime breaking ties with Israel was anti-Semitism which had brought a curse on Zambia. Sichone and Chikulo argue that:

> Born again Christians have long championed the cause of the state of Israel which they confuse with the biblical tribe of Judah. Kaunda did not accept their claim that Zambian economy was in decline because Zambia did not have diplomatic relations with Israel but Chiluba government is eager to re-establish ties with Israel while showing open hostility to Islamic states and also accepts the pro-capitalist ideology of American churches with enthusiasm.

To redress Zambia's diplomatic relations with Israel, Chiluba had to re-dedicate the country back to God based on 2 Chronicles, 7:14: "If my people who bear my name humble themselves, and pray and seek my presence and turn from their wicked ways, then I will listen from heaven and forgive their sins and restore their country." Zambia was declared a Christian nation so that God would bless the nation. This dedication was inserted in the preamble of the constitution of the republic. It is from this religious background that Chiluba and the MMD started their reign in the early 1990s. Chiluba, the MMD and the Zambian masses had a common enemy; Kaunda, UNIP and humanism. In order to return the country on the road to economic, political and social development these presumed vices were to be got rid of. As Michael Bratton notes in *Journal of Democracy:*

> Equally troubling are indications of lack of deep popular attachment to democratic values. There was, after all, mass celebration in response to the erroneous news of Kaunda's ousting during the aborted coup attempt of June 1990. This suggests that Zambians were willing to

accept any form of political change -democratic or not- as long as it resulted in the removal of a leader who had overstayed his welcome.

It can be concluded from Bratton's assertion that Zambians favored multi-partism, being the only alternative at the moment, thinking that freedom in its variety would grant the country economic development and liberate the people from dependency on the government.

The Zambian transition to multi-party democracy was a peaceful process due to Kaunda's genuine acceptance to the demands of the masses. The MMD managed to capture the masses support due to its vibrant manifesto, which reflected the people's deepest needs. The MMD promised to create a free market economy, which would empower the Zambian people to run their own economy.

During the first, third republic, democratic elections in 1991 the MMD won with a landslide because people no longer had confidence in UNIP. The MMD was the only party that could provide opposition. Ironically, the MMD and Chiluba's government had overwhelming ideas but its members were the same old politicians who had served in the UNIP government. There were thirty or so registered political parties most of which were weak and unable to provide substantial opposition.

The MMD had a manifesto, which expressed Zambia's greatest need for reform. In 1991 during the election campaign the MMD and the people of Zambia agreed to work together towards reform. People knew that the reform program was not an easy process yet they believed in the MMD and were ready to participate in it through different established democratic institutions. The MMD had promised to create employment by encouraging new investors; both foreign and local. The reform policy outlined its objectives of improving the economy by privatization, the free market, and structural adjustment program. Ihonvbere notes that the objectives of the 1993 recovery program were tight. He outlines some of the immediate measures as:

Reduction in the domestic borrowing by government and the parastatals; bringing inflation down to 10 percent; abolishing supplementary appropriations to government ministries; repaying much of government's outstanding debt to the banking systems; freeing up resources for private sectors expansions, and running the government on a cash basis.

This program had been no other than the demands of the donor communities, the World Bank, and the IMF of which Chiluba had pledged allegiance to. The quest to implement the structural adjustment program led the MMD to shun their mandate for accountability to the electorate who had promised to corroborate in the reform. Instead the MMD became puppet to the International donor communities.

The MMD through the reform program at least managed to reform the following sectors: health, education, and transport. Also the dilapidated infrastructure was repaired and the Zambian people were given much confidence in determining their own destiny through a free market economy. Nonetheless, it is sad to note that many Zambians were financially crippled to take up the challenge of investment and the running of private business.

The MMD was fully confident that the privatization process would be a success and that new investors would storm the country hence creating more employment and empowerment of the people. Unfortunately, the privatization of the public sector landed the country into massive retrenchments of the work force. The continue credit squeeze and the introduction of Value Added Tax (VAT) on imported goods restricted investors into the country.

Unemployment and lack of investment opportunities forced the people to resort to crime and unscrupulous transactions. Government ministers and party officials were getting richer and richer while the ordinary Zambians were growing poorer. As the saying goes, "the Zambian masses tightened their belts whilst ministers were adding more pieces to their belts."

In the political arena there seemed to be no stronger opposition to the MMD government. At the end of Chiluba's reign, the MMD had actually regressed to the Kaunda's form of governance. Any form of opposition within the ruling party implied disloyalty and accrued to disassociation from the party. Chiluba's early supporters and benefactors like the late Dean Mug'omba, Roger Chongwe, Kawimbe and Ben Mwila lost their alliance to the party because of being forceful and challenging to the government. In fact they all were cabinet ministers. Bratton questions the validity of democracy in Zambia when he notes that, "while the political transition was rapid, it remains fragile. In Zambia, newly independent political institutions and fledging democratic values do not yet form a permanent buffer against abuse by executive authority."

Today, when one looks at Zambia, one would begin to wonder if really democracy is a reality. This question could be triggered perhaps when one analyses what prompted the amendment of the national constitution in 1996. Was it not that the MMD and Chiluba were afraid that if they did not manipulate the constitution in their favor, Kaunda and UNIP would roll back to power? Again after ten years of governance Chiluba showed signs of betraying the Zambian people by trying to campaign for the amendment of the section in the constitution that restrict an incumbent president to two terms of office. What Chiluba wanted, by opting for a third term, is actually the very thing that he had condemned Kenneth Kaunda for over staying in power.

In what was foreseen as a way of revamping the economy; the MMD had privatized nearly 97% of parastatals only to realize that it was a great mistake that placed the country machinery of economy in foreign hands. It has been until recently that the Zambian government decided to retract the ownership of companies by liberalization of the business sector instead of privatization. This form of approach has great advantage over privatization because the government would still remain with some shares in major companies that have an impact on the country's economy.

Perhaps the only sign that indicates that democracy is at play in the Zambian society is that despite the weak opposition in the political Arena the social organizations, civic societies and religious organizations fully participate in promoting and safe-guarding the rule of law. People from all quarters are able to come together to air their views on matters of interest to the nation, for instance opposing the case of Chiluba seeking third term.

Conclusion

In practice both Zambian humanism and the declaration of Zambia as Christian nation failed to help the two governments; under scrutiny, to better the lot of the human person. Benedict XVI in *Caritas in Veritate* (Charity in Truth) acknowledges this reality that development of the human person has not changed in the world. The failure has not been that these two ideological and religious inclinations are inadequate but that the forms of governance undertaken by the two systems of government were not compatible with the ideological and religious inclinations the claimed to espouse. Kaunda had diverted from the true ideals of Zambia Humanism formulated within the concept of family that placed man and woman (person) at the centre of development. Unfortunately, in the final analysis it was only one man that had become the centre of development. The system of governance and the manipulation of Zambian Humanism had become so oppressive on the Zambian masses such that both Kaunda, UNIP and the ideology itself were despised. Chiluba's model of Christianity was fundamentalist in nature and dwelt on 'personal' prosperity. It supported more individualistic tendencies rather than the family values of Christianity that promotes love for neighbour. With its capitalist flavour, the declaration of Zambian as a Christian nation only propelled prosperity for the few elite in the ruling class living the masses in abject poverty. Though the Chiluba regime had given back confidence to the Zambian people to fend for themselves fewer were capable of doing that. The economic situation was not favourable for Zambians to participate in the economy through local investment. The few who were capable to participate in the economy did so either because they received favours from the Chiluba government. Corruption had become the order of the day and a clear mockery to the declaration of Zambia as a Christian nation. It suffices here to conclude with Benedict XVI's observation:

The theme of integral human development takes on an even broader range of meanings: the correlation between its multiple elements requires a commitment to foster the interaction of the different levels of human knowledge in order to promote the authentic development of peoples.

There is a common adage that goes, "the wealth of a nation is known by the quality of life of its people." All kinds of development ought to aim at the integral human development. As democracy is said to go with development it means the democratization of many African states ought to indicate developmental advancement. As for Zambia the reign of Kaunda and Chiluba is now history but it remains to the new regimes and the generations to come to see to it that the democratization of the country begins to reap benefits especially in terms of the integral development of the human person.

Questions for reflection:

1. Why is it important for a media house to have designated political reporters for the presidency?
2. Most presidential spokesperson are known to be masters of rhetoric and spin doctors. Why do you think people in society are skeptical of such an office?

Chapter Twenty-Three
Africa and the Cinema of Revolution

The Cinema of Revolution is one of the trends in African cinema that sets to document Africa's history of struggle and quest for autonomy rule during the colonial era. The filmmakers of the cinema of revolution, both indegineous and expartriats, dwell on the theme of the liberation struggle attempting to capture the intricacies of colonialism and the ideologies behind imperialism. The cinema of revolution, especially those concerning Africa, depict scenes that bring to the fore many humanitarian abuses on the rights of persons and society and how the international bodies fail or refuses to intervene in the internal affairs of nations in conflict. They also manage to bring up the whole issue of colonial discourse, though subversively, the imperialist quest to dominate other cultures. This is carried about by the ideology of hegemony and the West's attempt to universalise its world-view and place others as sub-cultures.

Introduction:

Three African cinemas of revolution, *The Battle of Algiers* (1957) by Gillo Pontecorvo, *Flame* (1986) by Ingrid Sincair and *Mapantsula* (1987) by Oliver Schmidtz and Thomas Mogotlane were all made few years before or after independence and were not shown in the countries they represent. The common humanitarian abuses in these cinemas of revolution are torture, child (soldiers) participation, women participation, crime, terrorism, civilian attacks and the role of the UN in the conflicts of rebellion and revolution. This essay under the heading of 'The Cinema of Revolution' will analyse 'The Battle of Algiers,' 'Flame' and 'Mapantsula' in an effort to establish their contemporary relevance and resonance.

Firstly, the essay shall give a synopsis of each of the three cinemas of revolution under consideration and their background. Secondly, it shall site and discuss issues of torture, child (soldiers) participation, women participation, crime, terrorism, civilian attacks, hegemony, and the role of the United Nations in the conflicts of rebellion and revolution and try to locate their relevance and resonance to the contemporary world. These humanitarian issues are interlinked hence they shall be discussed in their relatedness and not each as a particular topic were necessary. And thirdly, the essay shall argue for the strengths and limitations of African cinema of revolution and offer a position on the discourse of African cinema.

Film Synopsis:

The Battles of Algiers tells a story of the French occupation of Algeria and the Algerian's rebellion through the FLN resistance movement in the 60's. It tells the story through the character of La Pointe and Maussual. In the movie the French failure to counter the rebellion sees the police service being replaced by the French military. The movie is balanced in offering both sides of the story. It neither glorifies the French military nor the Algerian population. It is not that 'The Battles of Algiers offers an indelible image of how that boomerang pitilessly returns, which we ignore at our peril.'

It has scenes of torture, innocent children being bombed, Arab women disguised to plant bombs in the French quotas, a boy fully active in the FLN strategy to rebel against the French colony, the police being attacked and shot at by unsuspected Arabs.

Flame tells a story of two girls Nyasha - Liberty and Florence- Flame, from a rural background, with opposite longings, join the liberation struggle playing their roles, just as their male counterparts, but who fifteen years later are not recognised. Ingrid Sinclain the producer and writer of Flame states that her intention to make Flame was as a result of wanting to document the role of women in the struggle whose contributions to the war of liberation had long been forgotten. This observation echoes on the issue of women's contributions being sidelined during the post-independence era. Equally Flame reflects the issue of humanitarian violations such the involvement of child soldiers, bombings, corporal punishment, rape and unrecognised ex-combatants.

Mapantsula is a movie that locates a tsotsi's (thug)life ruled by harassing white women by stealing from them and his insensitivity to the life of struggle around him. It also shows the humanitarian violations such as the use of torture by the prison authorities to interrogate victims and use of military force on civilians to counter the revolution.

Indeed, The Battles of Algiers brings home the reality of child martyrs, interrogation rooms and torture chambers, the bombings in which innocent civilians from both sides are killed. "Sequence where three Algerian women plant bombs at various crowded hangouts in the French quarters. Masquerading as loose-living Europeans, carrying mortality in a shopping basket, they would be sinister femmes' fatales in another context" (1996:10). These are the same methods that terrorist 'suicide bombers' in the Israel-Palestinian war use against each other. In the American inversion of Iraq, the Iraqis used the same tactics to attack American soldiers.

In The Battles of Algiers we have the French counter attack in the Rue Caton 4 when they bomb the hide-out (Fatiha's house) of the FLN.

> Let's say first that movies have an accessory and not a decisive usefulness in various events and elements that contribute to the transformation of society …Political films are useful on one hand, if they contain a correct analyses of reality, and on the other, if they are made in such a way to have that analyses reach the largest possible audience (1996:52).

A Torture scene sets as the opening scene of The Battles of Algiers. An unshaven old Algerian is being interrogated through the use of torture to reveal the names of those who are engineers of the insurgencies. Another scene of torture is when La Pointe is in prison, sharing the same cell with FLN members, he witnesses a convict being guillotined. The most gruesome of all scenes of torture in the Battles of Algiers is when the French soldiers use all forms of torture such as electrocution, fire and water against civilians who take part in the demonstrations that erupts towards the end of the movie.

In the war against terror waged by the Americans a similar scenario of use of torture on the suspected terrorists had caused alarm in the international community. The use of torture is meant to dehumanise and incapacitate someone also as a method to instill fear in the masses. The psychology of torture is that it leaves an individual later on traumatised and unable to fight for his or her rights.

The civil war in Sudan between the government of Sudan (GoS) and Sudan Liberation Army (SLA) documents the atrocities of war on the civilians and the use of torture by both factions. "Sustained attacks by the government forces and the local Arab militias on the local civilian population have led to catastrophic levels of violence and distraction" (2004:4).

- Attempts to crush the insurgency using aerial bombardment, militia forces and regular armed forces-
- Armed groups with no basic command and control structure terrorise local population, committing rape, extra judicial killings arbitrary arrests, robbery and arson (2004:5).

Officers from military intelligence and militia leaders (Janjaweed) arrested 168 people all belong to the Fur tribe, 5-7 March 2004 and then summarily executed them at the security offices in Delaij, Wadi Salih province, western Darfur state. The arrests took place in the village of Zaray, Fairgo, Tairgo and Kaskildo, all South of Garsilla, Wadi Salih province. They were detained for alleged involvement with the Sudan Liberation Army (SLA) and taken to the security offices in Dalaij, a village 30 kilometres east of Garsilla town, Wadi Salih province. During their detention the 168 people were allegedly subjected to torture and summarily executed by firing squad" (SOAT Press Release: 6 April 2004: 1).

In Uganda the present government has been reluctant to phase torture by the army against civilians. It has been observed that "the use of torture as tool of interrogation is foremost among an escalation in human rights violations by Ugandan security and military forces since 2001" (2004:4).

Reasons for torture:

- political suppression;
- force victims to confess to links to the government's past political opponents or current rebel groups (2004:4).

Forms of torture:

Tying of hands and feet behind the victim and suspension from the ceiling of the victims, 'Liverpool' water torture – forcing the victim to lie face up, mouth open, under a flowing water spigot, severe and repeated beatings with the metal or wooden poles; cables; hammers and sticks with nails protruding, pistal-whipping, electrocution, male and female genital and body mutilation, death treats, strangulation, restraint; isolation, and verbal abuse and humiliation (2004:4).

> The prisoners alleged they were tortured in the Gulu fourth division army barracks detention centre, where they were subjected to ill treatment and torture there, held in this room for two weeks with no light and insufficient food, and the only female prisoner was gang-raped (2004:45)

The second issue identified in the cinemas of revolution is the presence of children. In Flame Florence-Flame and Nyasha- Liberty are both seventeen-year-old girls who are supposed to be in school but circumstances force them to join the liberation struggle. In The Battle of Algier the boy who brings the letter to La Pointe and reads for him plays a significant role in the struggle too. He is seen during the strike as selling news papers and echoing with delight the 'we have done it' (referring to the strike), the boy is again noticed interrupting the PA system which the French use to dissuade, in the casbas, civilians from demonstrating. The boy uses the PA to encourage the Algerians to go on with the strike and never to give up. In Mapantsula we see the young girl, supposedly the daughter of Mama doing the toi-toi dance before the government forces. The presence of children in conflicts as full players has been made even worse in modern times with child soldiers in the civil strife in Uganda, Sierra Leone and Angola.

> I was taken away in 1999 when I was 13 years old. At first, I was used to transport arms, supplies, and other materials. There were other children in our group, about 30. We were soon given training on how to fight. We shot with AK-47's and other weapons. I was the youngest in my troop of about 70, children and adults. We were on the front lines and I was sick, with bouts of malaria and often not enough to eat. I was in the troop only because they captured me in the first place. This wasn't my decision (Manoel P. former UNITA child soldier: testimony to the Human Rights Watch, 3rd December 2002).

Chapter Twenty-Four
Rhetoric as an Aid to Modern Advertisement

Communication is essential in every human endeavour; hence its theories enhance its effectiveness. Socrates, as introduced by Plato's *Gorgias*, formulates the theory of rhetoric based on the speech model of communication. Plato's work highlights the fact that rhetoric is "knowledge about words," therefore, an art of persuasion. In the contemporary world of communication and business the art of persuasion plays a major role in order to win clients to buy into one's ideas or products. Rhetoric can still be relevant in solving our communication problems today just as it were in the times of Socrates. It appeals to our contemporary fast moving world of information, communication and technology (ICT) in the sense that it has actually become difficult to grab the attention of the media savvy audiences. Having the ability of persuasion that rhetoric offers is the only assurance of success in this environment where media consumers are bombarded with information moving at a supersonic speed at every possible moment.

Advertisement is about selling of the product to would-be-consumers of our media products from whatever platforms we utilize to convey our messages. In doing advertisement we are actually packaging our message for the media consumer. With the advancement of technology and the multiplicity of media platforms the consumer is overwhelmed with myriads of images and messages aiming at changing his/her attitude by enticing him/her to buy the product. This fast-paced community of media savvy individuals has its own weaknesses. For instance, the problem of electronic communication whereby the overabundance of information that consumers are bombarded with are often poorly presented and never put in context to the extent that they lack significance or meaning. Consequently, no one takes them seriously. The problem today for those in marketing and advertising is how to capture the attention of the media savvy consumer. Why should he/she listen or read or watch your media package as advertiser among many other advertisers? Why should he/she take your message seriously and ignore the rest? This is where the art of rhetoric comes into play. An advertisement itself, as a media commodity, should be packaged according to the rules of the theory of rhetoric, especially its three-tier categories; namely *ethos* (Character of the presenter/speaker), *logos* (quality of massage), and *pathos* (appeal to the emotions of the audience).

The media today continue, based on the character of the speaker, to utilize the old tradition of having models or celebrities as surrogate mothers in advertisements. There are many such examples like the image of Lady Gaga in a marketing video of a Lexus car or using her name as a brand of an exorbitant perfume. In the same way, the image of Jennifer Lopez or Usain Bolt provides credibility that enhances the profile of the product to the consumer. Most adverts online and electronic, for instance those promoting good health habits, are demonstrating that knowledge is power and that it is not only the character of the speaker that matters but also the quality of the message. These advertisement provide a well-researched set of information that would appeal to an average consumer. Its presentation reinforces the image of the model or celebrity as being smart. The graphic images used in these advertisements and the language, as well as the image of the speaker, is such that they appeal to the emotions of the consumer. The default however is that, though the massage and the images portray knowledge, truth is often compromised.

In Zambia most of the adverts produced for the electronic media are usually packaged with humouristic appeals by using well-known comedians. Most often the message being communicated is less challenging or persuasive due to the lack of necessary information about the product. Hence, the element of providing knowledge to the targeted-would-be-consumer on the product is negated. The choice of comedy in advertisements works quite well in winning the attention of the viewers but it does not often guarantee greater sells of the commodity advertised. And also it isolates a majority of viewers, especially the affluent, who find most of the comedic display very myopic and childish. Worse still, most of these adverts tend to be longer than expected. Adverts are meant to be shorter, catchy and straight to the point especially if images are well selected to create a quick impression on the viewer or would-be-consumer.

The theory of rhetoric could inform producers of media advertisement in coming up with work that applies images of personalities that exude confidence and are credible, a message that provides informative data, and appeals to emotions and affinities of a variety of consumers. Source credibility is very important in a communication situation. Most advertisements have used personalities like of the first republican president of Zambia Kenneth Kaunda. For instance, prior to presidential elections to encourage voters to use their votes wisely. Credibility plays on making the would-be-consumer change his/her attitude towards the product and begin regarding the advert with a degree of seriousness.

Rhetoric seeks the most effective way of persuasion. In our contemporary world people are busy and pay less attention to electronic messages unless they are well packaged and appeal to their emotions, have credible sources and provide valuable information that adds knowledge to the would-be-consumer. Therefore, the theory of rhetoric, which is the art of persuasion, can lessen the nightmares that advertisers, marketing and public relations officers of modern times are subjected to in order to win consumers.

Questions for reflection:

1. How would you apply the communication theories you have learnt to modern day advertisement?
2. Do you think advertisements you have seen, watched or heard appeal to everyone in the same way? If yes or no, how?
3. What would be the best advertisement design for your generation for a media product such a smartphone?
4. What are the best adverts for you among the following; audio, visual or both? Explain your answer.

Chapter Twenty-Five
Parable of talents

This paper is going to discuss a story parable of Talents which is in Matthew 25: 14-30. This Parable of Talents is similar to that of the Parable of the Pounds in Luke 19:11-17. The essay will discuss the meaning of the parable, its historical; geographical and literary setting. It will also give the structural analysis and parallelism of the parable. It shall then state the significance of the parable for us today and also its theological implication.

Jesus during his public ministry taught people by mainly using parables. Archibald Hunter notes that more than one thirds of Jesus' teachings were in parables. This literary form of conveying his teachings on many issues made him a great teacher. In Judaism, just like in many African cultures and traditions, using figurative speech is regarded as a rich form of conveying ones message. For instance, in Bemba culture in order to advise someone on a wrong doing or unbecoming behaviour one has to be told in words warped with hidden meaning instead of coming out straight. The Jewish culture was rich in symbolism and imagery hence communication was endowed with these characteristics. Hence, Jesus used parables for a purpose of quickening 'understanding, by putting truth in a vivid and challenging and memorable way.' He used parables to teach about hidden truths. Most parables of Jesus were kingdom parables or eschatological sermons. Jesus used the parables to teach about certain facts about hidden reality such as the kingdom of God and the end of time. He told his parables through application of familiar realities to express or to illustrate the unknown. Hunter notes about the parables of Jesus that,

> Every parable of Jesus was meant to evoke a response and strike for a verdict. 'What do you think?' he sometimes begins, and where the

words are not found, the question is implied. There follows, as a rule, a true-to-life story to the urgent issues of the Kingdom of God, which is the theme of all the parables.

Title: The Parable of the Talents could also be called the story of the faithful and unfaithful servants or the Parable of God's Justice and human social responsibility.

I like the Parable of the Talents because I believe that as a creature of God I have a social responsibility towards fellow creatures. By being placed on earth I am being called to good stewardship of the other created things. It is through good stewardship that I can fully praise and reverence God. When I look at my life here on earth and that of others it is clear to me that life has a purpose. The fact that all life comes from God indicates that we creatures are like stewards entrusted with property for the master. Whatever we do we do it for the Lord. Our reward will be to share in the joy of the Lord.

The other reason why I like the Parable of the Talents is that it is a very controversial parable that can be misunderstood sometimes. What excites me about the imagery of the parable is the idea of investing what is given in order to make profit. The business like nature of the story captures my attention because I think I am more inclined to a business mindedness in my approach to life. That is making the best of what I have or rather improving on what is there.

a) Meaning of Parable of Talents:

The parable has resonance of entrepreneurship. That is to say Christians are called to commit themselves to the maximization of the Christian enterprise. To talk of entrepreneurship is not in the way we would understand it in the corporate sense but rather entrepreneurship in the sense of being ambassadors for Christ, people who have given themselves in the advancement of the kingdom of God. The committed are those who are "most effective and efficient with their time and opportunities to spread the good news of Christ." It means Christians who are faithful to their calling and are able to invest their lot for the sake of the kingdom. These are people who sacrifice their energies, creativity and innovativeness and surmount barriers that hinder others to become productive for Christ. It is to these people that Ephesians 5:16 and Colossians 4:5 speak to that "make the most of every opportunity." That means those who are fully dedicated to the cause of Christ will be rewarded and those who are unfaithful and show less commitment will be condemned.

In this parable the three servants are given different talents and the first two who doubled their talents are praised for their success and their faithfulness whilst the third servant is castigated for his failures and unfaithfulness. This means that Christians are expected to be faithful in their different areas of responsibility. They are supposed to be enterprising faithful servants. The parable teaches that Christians have all different abilities one from another. However, the Christian enterprise offers equal opportunity to be enterprising for Christ despite having different abilities and responsibilities. The meaning of the parable is that God has bestowed upon each individual abilities and everyone is obliged to fully develop his/her special gifts which have been graciously grated to them in order that it may be productive.

Setting of Parable:

Historical Setting: The original audience to this parable would not have had to allegorize the parable to make sense of it. Its portrait of a great household was all too familiar to them. The powerful master would often go away on an economic or political business. His affairs would be handled by slaves/servants, who in Roman society often rose to prominent positions in the household hierarchy as stewards. The sum entrusted here borders on hyperbole. Talent was one of the largest values of money in the Hellenistic world. One talent was equal to 6,000 denarii. A pound or a minas is worth $20.00 whilst a talent is worth $1,000.00 each. One denarius was an average subsistence wage for a day's labour, one talent was worth more than fifteen years wages.

Geographical Settings:

From the plot that the master was on a journey and he called his servants we can deduce that this was outside Palestine. In Palestine the work was performed by hired workers whereas outside Palestine it was performed by slaves or servants. Outside Palestine masters owned servants. Jesus must have told this parable on his way to Jerusalem because his disciples believed that the kingdom of God would come before they reached Jerusalem.

Literary Settings:

Immediate setting: David Flusser notes that in European languages the word 'talent' meant person's ability. In the parable we are told 'each was given to his own ability.' The term 'talent' in the parable refers to money. The master was very much aware of each servant's abilities and aptitude. It seems that the metaphoric application of the word 'talent' was derived from the ingenious interpretation of Proverbs 3:9, "Honour the LORD with your wealth, with first fruits of all your produce." It is the Lord who has graciously granted one these produce hence the need to offer the Lord as thanks-giving. This interpretation of proverbs fits with the moral teaching of the parable. The object of the parable in the Jewish setting is that the proprietor entrusts property to others with the hope that they would return it in an improved or developed state. The third servant thought that returning it in the original state would be sufficient. He ignored his duty to repay the owner the sum with interest. It is his failure that brought punishment on him. The final repayment is the significant point in the deep meaning of the parable. The proprietor symbolizes God, "and the entrustment of property means a gracious loan from Him, being entrusted yet never a possession of ours at our discretion." Matthew highlights the fact that fear or 'little' faith will keep people from true discipleship. The fear of the unfaithful servant serves as a warning against that attitude.

The recognition of human diversity and abilities is typically Matthean. Faithful servant means trustworthy and risk-taking.

Wide context: The Parable of the Talent is part of the eschatological discourse that begins from Matthew 24:1-25:46. The Parable of the Talents belongs to the series of judgment parables. Matthew concludes Jesus' discourse teaching with the judgment parables. It appears before the story of the Last Social Judgment and immediately after the parable of the Ten Bridesmaids or Ten Virgins. Matthew chapter 24 and 25 shows the compassion heart of Jesus and love mingled unwavering holiness. The eschatological discourse constitutes warnings, prophecies, and encouragements to His people Israel prior to His departure. Jesus the Lord is leaving for undisclosed period of time. He is delegating to them the responsibilities, as stewards, to care for His kingdom. The parable of the Talents impresses on them the weight of that responsibility and the serious consequences of neglecting to understand and apply is instructions. This message can also be extended to all mankind. The

Parable of the Ten Virgin ends with the phrase "therefore, stay awake, for you know neither the day nor the hour" (Mt25:13). It is from here that the Parable of the Talents picks up, thus "it will be like when a man who was going on a journey and called his servants...." (Mt25:14).

The master knew the abilities of each of the servants and as it were the servants knew also the personality and character of their master. The Lord knows the abilities of each of his stewards and the stewards know the character and personality of their Lord. The Lord expects them to know Him very well and enough to apply the spirit as well as the letter of His instructions. Those who do so are richly rewarded and those who fail receive severe judgment. The stewards who make profit are praised and given increased responsibilities and invited to enter into the joy of the Lord. The untrusting steward is scolded, rejected and punished.

The application of this parable must be understood within the context of message of Matthew 24-25. It is first the message to the people of Israel that will live in the last days before the Lord returns. Matthew 24:13-14, "But the one who perseveres to the end will be saved. And this gospel of the kingdom will be preached throughout the world as witness to all nations, and then the end will come" is a key statement. This is the believing remnant that will receive the promise of the kingdom. There is also a universal application to all mankind.

Immediate Setting: The New Jerome Biblical Commentary notes about the Parable of the Talents that, "in its present context it offers a life-style for the interim before the Son of Man returns, urging us to a responsible use of the master's goods in view of the judgment to come." This parable of Jesus was told to illustrate an aspect of the nature of the kingdom of God. For Christians, diligence in carrying out one's responsibilities is essential for more important tasks in the future. Jesus engaged his listeners in his parables to make them think about God's justice and their social responsibility.

Analysis of Parable:

The Parable of the Talents utilizes the rule of repetition. However, the stress should fall on the end. The stress is on the episode of the third servant who hid the talent. "So that it would be unfair to say that the two successful characters are only there in the story as foils to this 'barren rascal.'" The parable communicates comparatively praise and blame while emphasis is laid on the third servant who failed to put to use the talent he had received. The man of the story is the third servant who has qualities of a whistle blower: "Master, I knew you were a demanding person, harvesting where you did not plant and gathering where you did not scatter…" (Mt 25: 24). The man of the story is not an exemplary character but one who is afraid to take risks, one who is not moved to positive action for fear of the master. This knowledge of the character and personality of his master instead of inspiring the third servant to more creativity and innovativeness it, as it were, crippled him. The pouch-line of the story is the interaction between the master and the third servant. It is in this character that the story reaches its climax.

The journey of the master or merchant is an allegory of Christ, his journey has become ascension, and his subsequent return has become the Parousia, which ushers his own into the Messianic banquet.

Parallelism: The Parable of The Talents in Matthew 25:14-30 is similar to the Parable of the Pounds in Luke 19:11-27. In the Parable of the Pound the servants are given the same amount of money to invest whereas in the Parable of the Talents each is given according to his ability. Also the number of servants is different when being given the money, ten in the Parable of the Pound and three in the Parable of the Talents. In both parables we hear of three servants being called to account for what was given them and the story unfolds in a similar manner. The first two servants in both parables increase their allotment by 100% whilst the third servant stored the money either in the handkerchief or buried it in the ground. The number of servants is three and the number three is a typical pattern in parables and similar literary forms. Usually the number is used to in order to create a gradation. In both parables there is a descending gradation. Three different persons represent in the simplest way the variety of human abilities. The plot of the Parable of the Talents is built upon the contrast of only two protagonists, the positive and the negative hero. The parable has a tripartite structure which gives a contrast between two opposites. Luke has added the element of the man on a journey as someone seeking the throne of kingship a part that Matthew omits in his parable.

Structure: The parable can be broken down in these events:

- The man going on a journey
- The Journey
- The man's return

- The servants
- Each servants ability
- The talents
- The investments (how the talents are invested)
- The profits (what these are, and how they can be measured)
- Burial of the talent
- Rewards

The crisis points in the story are shown by the dialogue that takes place between the master and the servants. Thus the tripartite structure can be expressed in the following categorization of the parable:

i. 14-19 Includes the masters departure and the actions of the servants:
ii. 20-23 Episodes of reckoning with the two faithful servants: Repetition of the story and the master's reward.

> "Master, you gave me ….talents. See, I have made …more." His master said to him, 'Well done, my good and faithful servant. Since you were faithful in small matters, I will give you great responsibilities. Come, share your master's joy."

iii. 24-28 Reckoning with the unfaithful servant.

Significance of the Parable of Talents for us today:

I would agree with Perkins when he notes that, "the ability to take responsibility and risk is vital part of our well-being and growth as humans." Risk taking is a way towards success. We should avoid fear if we are to achieve anything in life. Fear makes us act in an inappropriate way causing us miss on opportunities that come our way. They say it is better to be counted among those who tried and failed rather than among those who never tried at all. It took a scientist 199 times of failure to discover the firmament in an electric bulb. In our age we know that scientists are still making uncountable number of researches in order for them to find a cure for HIV/AIDS. The many times that others have failed does not stop upcoming scientist from venturing into research. Knowledge is power. Therefore, putting our knowledge to good use is what is going to attain us success.

Theological Reflection:

Each human being has been entrusted with resources of time and material wealth. Everything under the earth comes from God. Each human being is responsible for using those resources so they can increase in value. Christians have additionally the most valuable resource of all –the Word of God. They will be accountable to the Lord for the use of His resources. Perkins argues that our Christian calling "also involves the risk of exposing ourselves and what we believe to the give and take challenge by others. Such dialogue, challenge and open hostility were part of the experience of every Christian in the time of the evangelists."

This parable of Jesus is a true story and not a real story. If it were a real story one would question how the first two servants managed to double their talents in a period of a man's journey. Perhaps the man of our story was scared to invest the money because he might have been afraid to incur a loss and it was only wise for him to think of returning the money in its original state. However, this aspect of the story about the ethics of the story was less important. The story worked well for Jesus' audience because this humanly story as fictitious as it were was able to convey the message about eminent going of the Lord and His eventual Parousia.

Conclusion:

This essay has attempted to demonstrate that the Parable of the Talents is in the group of the eschatological discourse of Jesus and that it had significant lessons to teach to his audience about the kingdom of heaven. It has also to explain the parable through the historical, geographical and literary setting. Through parallelism the essay has managed to show how the Matthean Parable of the Talents is similar and differs with the Lucan version in the Parable of the Pounds or Minas. The structural analysis has illustrated how Matthew has utilized the repetition motif and the comparisons of two protagonists or the positive and negative motif. And in the final analysis the essay has indicated that the Parable of the Talents has great significance to the people of today just as it had to Jesus' audience.

Chapter Twenty-Six
Forgiveness and Reconciliation

The year 1999 was declared the Year of Forgiveness by Pope John Paul II subsequently a decade later in 2009 the theme for the Second African Synod was: The Church in Africa in Service to Reconciliation, Peace and Justice. These themes by the Church indicate how important the issues of forgiveness and reconciliation have become for our world today on both the interpersonal and collective dimensions. When we look at our world today, the subject of forgiveness and reconciliation has become so necessary because of the hatred and animosity expressed through terrorism, ethnic conflict and the disintegration of family life and values in society. On a global level we are not short of examples that call for forgiveness and reconciliation when it comes to nations in conflict or under acts of terrorism and ethnic clashes.

In this world so deeply shaken by immerse individual and collective evil forgiveness and reconciliation is paramount provided justice is not neglected. Forgiveness and reconciliation can be engaged on different levels, on an individual and on a collective level. To address the needs for forgiveness and reconciliation at both individual and collective levels a multi-dimensional approach might be required. That is as an individual one can seek forgiveness from the self, from the other, from the community and from God. Collectively, they might seek forgiveness and reconciliation from themselves, from the others and from God.

Defining Forgiveness and Reconciliation:

The terms 'forgiveness' and 'reconciliation' can be described as two sides of the same coin. We cannot speak of reconciliation without the parties concerned having undergone through the process and experience of forgiving and forgiveness. It is this process and experience of forgiving and being forgiven that yields reconciliation. Therefore, forgiveness is a process in reaching the reconciled state. In other words, forgiveness, as a human action precedes reconciliation." Adrian Hastings in The Oxford Companion to Christian Thought describes reconciliation thus:

> Reconciliation in classical theology means much the same as redemption, atonement, or, even, salvation. It refers to the removal of division between God and humanity, a division brought by sin and overcome by Jesus Christ, both Son and God and new Adam, in whom divinity and humanity are reconciled (597).

Reconciliation here presupposes the state of sinfulness and the need for God. This understanding makes more sense when we talk of personal sinfulness and the desire to be reconciled with the self, the other and God. This aspect of reconciliation and forgiveness is what the Church caters for in the sacrament of reconciliation. Reconciliation and forgiveness at the communal level addresses social sin. At a higher level we can talk of reconciliation and forgiveness in terms of the cosmos. Here we are rather interested in individual and communal aspects of reconciliation and forgiveness.

Therapeutically, forgiveness and reconciliation heals memories of past traumatic experiences and enables one to look to the future with confidence. Scripture highlights this reality in James 5:16, "Confess your sins to one another that you may be healed." The experience of the sacrament of reconciliation bears testimony to this reality. Consequently, for a community as well appealing for forgiveness and reconciliation for a collective sin brings healing to the community and open doors for a new beginning. Lack of forgiveness and failure to reconcile cripples the victims as well as the culprits. Survivors of genocide or apartheid need to hear the perpetrators of these crimes confess their wrong doings, show remorse for their acts and if necessary be willing to face the wrath of justice. At the same time the victims or better survivors have to testify through sharing their traumatic experiences in order for them to receive the healing of memories. For the perpetrator, the willingness to seek for forgiveness and reconciliation also heals them and fortifies them to face the future with a free mind.

The sacramental dimension of reconciliation is very necessary for the believer whilst, the universal dimension is appropriate for settling world and ethnic conflicts. Forgiveness, as it were, is a choice or a decision made and this decision ought to be mutually reciprocated by the other party as well. Though forgiveness and reconciliation begin with the self, coming to terms with reality and having to arrive at a decision, it is much more an enterprise involving two parties or more. Therapists conquer that, for therapy to be successful, people first need to forgive themselves, for only then can they be able to forgive others. For Christians, the subject of forgiveness and reconciliation has both the sacramental and universal appeal. The universal appeal is inclusive of non-Christians as well and it is a universal longing.

Sacramental dimension of forgiveness and reconciliation:

In the decree of the Sacred Congregation for Divine Worship the sacrament of penance has been recognized as the sacrament of reconciliation. Reconciliation between God and men was brought about by our Lord Jesus Christ in the mystery of his death and resurrection (cf. Rom. 5:10). The Lord entrusted the ministry of reconciliation to the Church in the person of the Apostles (cf. 2 Cor. 5:18-21). The Church carries this ministry out by bringing the good news of salvation to men and by baptizing them in water and the Holy Spirit (cf. Mt. 28:19).

Forgiveness in the Christian sense entails that one realizes that s/he is a sinner and that s/he needs to reconcile with God. Seeking for forgiveness becomes a choice that one makes in order to be reunited with the creator. The element of sin is very important. One has to feel inadequate due to sin before the creator and hence seek for forgiveness in the sacrament of reconciliation. Wanting to reconcile with the creator is saying 'no' to sin and hence mending up the broken relationship that was caused by sinfulness. The parable of the prodigal son demonstrates the loving mercy of God, a God who forgives. Coming to one's senses and wanting to right the relationship with God could be a moment of conversion for one who previously had no inclination to follow the Christian way. Conversion then begins by renouncing one's sinfulness and professing Jesus as Lord and master of one's life. Baptism is actually a symbol of the experience of God's grace of forgiveness.

The Christian history is a history of salvation. Scripture is rich with examples of how people reconciled with God through the power of forgiveness. One example of a biblical reconciliation scene is the story of Jacob and Esau in Genesis 33: 1-14; 46:1-47:12. The motif of reconciliation underlies the book of

Hosea where the prophet obeys God's command to reunite with his faithless wife, Gomer. Psalms 51 echoes the plea for reconciliation at the personal level. Reconciliation between persons is a pattern as well in the ethical teaching of Jesus, for instance Matthew 5:23-26, He teaches about how one should first get reconciled with his or her brother before bringing sacrifice to the Lord. Then Galatians 6:1 talks of fraternal correction, which is a form of making peace with one another. In Mt 18:21-22 the importance of forgiveness is highlighted when Peter asks Jesus how many times must he forgive one who has wrong him. Jesus' reply of seventy-seven times tells about how forgiveness should be a constant thing without one getting fed-up with it. Forgiveness and reconciliation are meant to build up communities.

Basically, seeking for forgiveness and reconciliation from God in the sacrament is a great gift the Church gives to humanity. God is a major player in the individual dimension of forgiveness and reconciliation. Sin is mostly against God and against the other. It is in the penitential formula where emphasise is directed at the tripartite nature of sin. For instance, in the confessional one is expected to articulate the sins against God, neighbour and self so as to receive absolution. The universal dimension of forgiveness and reconciliation tries to address the sins committed against others, God, humanity and the cosmos.

The universal dimension of forgiveness and reconciliation:

The talk about forgiveness and reconciliation is not an easy one when it comes to looking at it from the universal perspective. Normally when we talk about the mitigation of conflicts, wars, terror and human negligence, the themes that emerge are justice and peace. The themes of forgiveness and reconciliation are usually down-played because they seem to deter justice and peace in the long run. For instance, in South Africa the Kairos document came out clear on this issue and articulated its fears of the process of reconciliation carried out by the Truth and Reconciliation Commission (TRC). The Kairos document notes that:

> The fallacy here is that 'Reconciliation' has been made into an absolute principle that must be applied to all cases of conflict or dissension… Reconciliation, forgiveness, and negotiation will become our Christian duty only when the apartheid regime shows signs of genuine repentance.

The fears expressed by the Kairos document are genuine. However, forgiveness and reconciliation must be viewed as necessities in the process of bringing justice and peace. The Pontifical Council for Justice and Peace, in its document called Compendium of the Social Doctrine of the Church, outlines how forgiveness and reconciliation would feat in the project of bringing justice and peace. In the document the council argues rightly that, "mutual forgiveness must not eliminate the need for justice and still less does it block the path that leads to truth. On the contrary, justice and truth represent the concrete requisite for reconciliation" (2004: 278). Justice will only be met when the offender acknowledges the mistake and assumes responsibility and henceforth would the process to reconciliation and forgiven be made light. The reservation to forgiveness and reconciliation makes it clear that the path to true forgiveness and reconciliation is not a smooth one. It is for this fact that Desmond Tutu dabbed the processes and achievement of reconciliation in South Africa as a miracle.

When we consider the Rwandan genocide of 1994 and the Kenyan post-election violence of 2007-2008 we would reckon that these nations would have by now addressed these past atrocities in an amicable way, but this is not the case. The trauma and the wounds are still fresh in the minds of its nationals. Rwanda has failed up to now to walk the route of South Africa, so does Kenya. These two nations have failed to address their past violence through engaging in the truth and reconciliation process where culprits voluntarily request for forgiveness and where the victims testifies and accept forgiveness. For South Africa the process and the actual reconciliation have had multiple effects on the growth of the nation. This for South Africa was the process of national healing. In Kenya there is still looming fears that the 2012 elections might be characterized by further ethnic animosity and violence.

Conclusion:

Our world today has been dented with both individual and collective sin on a large scale that threatens world peace. The echoes of justice and peace are heard everywhere where injustice and mayhem have taken root. More than ever before the world is punting for peace and peace it needs at all costs. Though at face value forgiveness and reconciliation seem as the cheapest way to the attainment of peace, these are the surest and safest modalities to bring justice and peace to our troubled world. On the individual dimension seeking for forgiveness and reconciliation pays to the individual who realizes his/her past mistakes and seeks to amend. For those who belong to the Church the sacrament of reconciliation is a moment of grace to experience the loving mercy of a forgiving father who seeks to reconcile with his children. All in all, to call for justice and peace, forgiveness and reconciliation should be the preconditions to their realization.

Chapter Twenty-Seven
Jesus Christ with a Zambian Face

This essay seeks to develop a Christology of the Zambian context using the methodology used by Peter Phan. Though Phan formulates a Christology of Asia prompted by Jesus' question "Who do you say that I am?" the actual problem he addresses is more anchored on Choan-Seng Song's (Theological Studies, 1996: 417) Christology. Song's Christology puts emphasis not on the identity of Christ but on whom Christ identifies with in the Asian context. In trying to formulate a Zambian Christology I would suppose a Zambian theologian would, like Song, address the question "Whom does Christ identify with in the Zambian context?" It is by responding to this question that it can be said a Zambian theologian has successfully defined Christ's identity. Phan argues that by taking this approach will the Christology being formulated make sense to the people in that given context. This is a Christology from below that has its praxis that is historical and constructed on the socio-economic, political and anthropological dimensions or experience of a given society. This is the same type of Christology advocated by Takatso Mofokeng in his article "Hermeneutical Explorations for Black Christology" (Parkee J, 1992). Mofokeng argues that:

> A relevant Christology arises, as we observed in the history of Christology, during moments of cleavages and cracks in the socio-economic, cultural and religious dimensions of social formations. It emerged at times when it is abundantly clear to all committed followers of the messiah from Nazareth, those who are eager to be at the cutting edge of world and human history, that their inherited theology which they held very dearly and protected very jealously against all ideological assaults is no longer able to explain events around them, nor to support

their faith or even to stimulate hope beyond the cleavages and cracks in society and church (1992: 85).

What can be deduced from Mofokeng's argument is that a theology and in particular a Christology that is relevant to a people should be one that finds resonance in their socio-economic, political, cultural and religious dimensions of their daily existence. Their practising of religious beliefs should be in touch with what they cleave for, what defines them and what moves them or make them tick as a people. When their Christology emerges to be out of sync with issues that worry them, challenges that they face then such a Christology is impotent, it has become like salt that has lost its saltiness. A Christology that emphasises the vertical dimension alone at the expense of the horizontal dimension gets relegated to oblivion. It's a pie in the sky; it doesn't fly. Theology and Christology in particular should take both a vertical and horizontal dimension. This task is beyond inculturation where, for instance, we pick elements of culture and tradition and infuse them into our faith. Sometimes, such an approach might still appear remote from the people's realities. You might include the cultural or traditional element in the Christian practise yet that is not what the immediate milieu is about. Such a traditional element; to the urban young, might revoke memories of elements in the remote past that have no relevance to the present. In our case we are talking of a Christology that is formulated from the Zambian context for it to be meaningful and relevant to the Zambian milieu. This will be the approach that this essay will try to synthesise in developing a Christology of Jesus Christ with a Zambian face.

Phan (1996) formulates a dualistic Christology of Asia by identifying the third-worldliness of Asia and also its religiosity. This dualistic Christology finds a meeting point in the praxis of liberation. The third worldliness has the ramifications of poverty, unemployment, crime, illiteracy, corruption which are brought about due to poor governance. Hence, Christ Jesus is identified with the suffering woman struggling with her children in the ghettos of Mumbai or Hong Kong, a homeless boy in Calcutta and a labourer in the factories of China. By identifying Christ with the suffering masses Phan advocates for a liberation theology that uplifts the livelihood of the suffering masses. The religiosity character of Asia is so unique to this part of the world. Bringing Christianity to this part of the world did not introduce religiosity to it. Therefore, Phan argues that for Christianity to be relevant to Asia it has to tap into the religious experience already in existence in this part of the world. He proposes that Christ Jesus has to be identified with the Buddhist monk's way of life that opts for a spirituality that liberates the spirit from the materialistic world. This simplicity of life is as a vehicle of fighting the social injustices that lead the masses to live in entrenched poverty. The Buddhist monk's life becomes a force that propels social change. Therefore, the religiosity of Asia is linked in some sense to the third-worldliness in terms of the praxis of liberation.

The Asian context is very different from that of Africa in the sense that the histories of these two continents are different though both share a common element of colonialism. In this sense it can be said that formulating a Christology of Zambia would be very different to the project of Phan. This essay will attempt at least to utilise the methodology of Phan to formulate a Christology of Zambia. It must be stated here that Phan's Christology is balanced in the sense that it has both a positive aspect as identified in the religiosity dimension and a negative aspect in the sense of third-worldliness. However, Mofokeng's articulation of a Black theology somehow highlights the darkest part of history; that of apartheid. We cannot run away from this reality as it is part of history. In formulating a Christology of Zambia it might seem unfortunate to highlight only the negative aspects. Jesus himself identified with the downtrodden and the underprivileged.

In responding to the question, whom does Christ Jesus identify with in the Zambian situation? I see two distinct responses. Firstly, in the socio-economic and political dimension, I see Christ Jesus identifying himself with people who have become destitute due to mass retrenchments of the labour force. Secondly, in the socio-cultural and spiritual dimension, I see Christ Jesus identifying himself with people afflicted by disease such as H.I.V/AIDS, malaria and tuberculosis. This dimension, in the traditional setting, brings suspicion of witchcraft. I am going to contextualise the above assumptions and show that both dimensions converge in a theology that constructs the praxis of liberation.

Zambia is one of the poorest nations of the world. With a population of about only 12 million; two thirds (68%) of its people live below the poverty line of $1per day. Zambia's economy was heavily dependent on copper. For over a decade now copper prices have fluctuated on the world market. With the ushering in of democracy in Zambia with liberal economic tendencies in the early 1990's most of the mines were privatised leading to a loss of jobs by thousands of employees. Most Zambians were not able to invest in mining because they lacked capital to do so. This meant that the government had to woe foreign investors to come and invest in the mining sector. Few employees were retained by the new investors causing doom to thousands who depended on the mines to earn their livelihood. One of the incentives the Zambian government had put in place to do this was to exempt foreign investors in the mining sector from paying tax for the first ten years of operation. To evade tax most foreign investors would fold up after the first ten years causing thousands of employees to be laid off. The fact that copper prices were not doing well on the world market meant that foreign investors were hesitant to come and invest in Zambia.

The collapse of the mines had a ripple effect on other industries that were dependant on the mines either as suppliers of services and materials or receivers of mining products. For instance, schools, hospitals and sports clubs that were run by the mines also got affected and were privatised. The electric company that supplied power to the mines also collapsed. The collapse of these industries led to mass retrenchments of the labour force. This meant unemployment to many Zambians living along the line of rail. As mining was the biggest earner of national income for the government followed by the tax collected from the labour force it meant that that revenue was no longer available. The government was not able to sustain the civil service hence it stopped recruiting graduating teachers, doctors, nurses and so forth. The government also had to lay off some employees in the civil service as it was no longer able to pay them. The ripple effect of the collapse of the mining sector on other industries and the civil service was so enormous. People in the cities, who before enjoyed many services provided by the government, were now destitute. Unemployment had become rampant as people were struggling to engage in small businesses to make ends meet.

All in all, the scenario described above of the collapse of the mining sector and its negative effects on the labour force indicate that many Zambians had become destitute encumbered by unemployment. In formulating a Christology that is relevant to the Zambian context this stark reality of poverty and unemployment has to be born in mind. Christ Jesus has to identify himself with the destitute living along the line of rail and elsewhere who struggle to find ways of surviving and make ends meet. This is the first praxis of formulating a Christology with Christ Jesus who has a Zambian face. The socio-economic and political dimensions of the Zambian situation call for a theology that constructs the praxis of liberation.

In the socio-cultural and spiritual dimension the Zambian context brings to light the issue of sickness and the suspicions that issues from it. Zambia as a developing nation has not been spared by the scourge of H.I.V/AIDS. About 17% of the population is infected and a larger number is affected by the pandemic. The sad reality is that most of those infected are in the productive age group; i.e 15 – 49 years, hence depriving many families of bread winners. The issue of H.I.V/AIDS requires concerted effort in order to be mitigated. The issues of stigma, prevention, treatment are very cardinal in addressing the scourge. How do the Zambian masses respond to the issue of H.I.V/AIDS? There are many levels at which this question can be addressed. There is the level of advocacy, care and research. In the context of theology a faith based response is offered in terms of advocacy and care. At advocacy level you can talk of proper treatment and increased funding for treatment, care and research. At care level you can talk of home based care carried out by faith based communities and civil communities.

Malaria and T.B are the biggest killers of people in Zambia, even exceeding that of H.I.V/AIDS. Here also there is the issue of funding and having good health facilities that are able to provide adequate health care to the already impoverished masses. At the core of providing good health facilities is the issue of governance. How committed his the Zambian government in providing health services to its poor communities? This is a very big problem because the government has wrong priorities. Every year when the minister of finance presents the budget to parliament the health issue does not surface as priority. For instance, the annual budgetary allocation for defence and security far exceeds that of health; even when we know that Zambia is a peaceful nation and unlikely to go to war at any time.

This scenario of health presents a case where many Zambians are left to die in remote areas due to lack of medication or better medical facilities. Even when medication is available people are poor to have nutritious diets that would enhance speedy recovery in case of T.B treatment. It is this scenario that provides ground for formulating a Christology of liberation. Because people are poor and the country has poor medical facilities, when faced with issues of H.I.V/AIDS, Malaria and T.B, people turn to apportioning blame on witchcraft. In times of such sicknesses people sort the help of witch doctors instead of conventional medicine. Christ Jesus needs to identify himself with a person languishing in the remote parts of Zambia with H.I.V/AIDS. Christ Jesus ought to identify himself with a poor woman in Shangombo ailing with T.B and at the same time unable to have good nutrition when on medication. Christ Jesus needs to identify himself with a poor boy in Likulu dying of malaria because the nearest health centre has neither personnel nor facilities for treating the disease. The question of governance comes here because medical personnel sometimes refuse to go and serve in remote parts of the country and also that their services are not well remunerated. Another issue is that the government does not see health as a priority. A theological response that is faith based is exemplified by mission hospitals in remote areas like Katete, Chikuni, Mpashya and others. It is also exemplified by the home based care projects that are found in most parts of the country as a response to the mitigation of H.I.V/AIDS and T.B.

In conclusion, the best response in which African Christologies can be contextualised is when it deals with the concrete situations of a people. In case of Zambia we are talking about the pertinent issues such as poverty, unemployment and disease. The Zambian government is mandated by law to provide employment, health care and address issues of poverty. Other institutions such as faith based and civil society are called to be partners in providing assistance in these areas. It is in this area that a theology of liberation is needed to speak on behalf of the afflicted, the unemployed and the poor. It needs to fight the social injustice that creates a pyramid in the socio-economic strata with a fraction living in immoral opulence, a sizeable number surviving in the middle class and a legion wallowing in abject penury. This reality is reflected when we juxtapose a well fledged corrupt minister or member of parliament driving a limousine and an emaciated security guard riding a bicycle to work. A theology built on the praxis of liberation will provide hope for the other Christ living or identified with the jobless, the hapless and the ailing.

This essay has tried to formulate a Zambian Christology that makes Christ Jesus have a Zambian face. It has done so in two ways; namely, the socio-economic and political dimension and the socio-cultural and spiritual dimension. It has identified that contextualising Christ Jesus in these two ways creates ground for the praxis of liberation, though this was not elaborated fully due to word-economy.

Chapter Twenty-Eight
Christmas and Children

Christmas is indeed a right time for celebration and renewal for all of us. We celebrate the birth of Jesus, God made man. As we commemorate the incarnation of the Son of Man who came to share his divine life with humanity and to establish the reign of God, we realize that this festive season is indeed a moment to share our love, joy, peace and justice with those around us, especially children.

Every year as we think and prepare for the coming of the Child Jesus we also should think of children all over the world. Some years ago the missionary intention for the month of December is for children and young people that they may be messengers of the Gospel and that they may be respected and preserved from violence and exploitation.

In preparation for Christmas we ought every time to think of the rights of children. Much more, those people who are blessed with happy families as they celebrate with their children they might also think of the many children who live in disadvantaged environments and in destitution. The period of Christmas opens an opportunity for us to share with the many disadvantaged children in our midst. The Child Jesus was born in a manger because there was no room for them in the inn (LK 2:7).

It is also right time that everybody in society reflected on the dignity of children and vowed to get committed to the promotion of children's rights. Parents and guardians and all citizens should work towards curbing violence and exploitation against children. The respect of children and preservation from violence and exploitation of children should begin with every nuclear and extended families and also institutions concerned with the plight of children.

Using force and violence as a mode of discipline is old fashioned and bizarre. Parents and guardians have an obligation to bring up children in the training and instruction of the Lord (Eph 6:4). During Christmas festive season parents and guardians should sacrifice working overtime, meeting with friends at recreation joints for their children. Parents and guardians should have time for their children to seat, talk, listen and play with them. Having quality time with our children and allowing them to express themselves is a first step towards respect for the dignity of children. What we say and do to children in their formative years is very important to them and it contributes to their forming a character. That is why it is important for adults to be role models to their children and other children in society. If we live and share our love in the family and with others and we promote a peaceful environment where justice prevails our children will be empowered to value these virtues.

During Christmas festive season we should all work towards forming a good character in children by appreciating, praising, rewarding, acknowledging and valuing them. We should not only think of our own children but those living in institutions such as orphanages and also in our streets. It is believed that children learn what they live. It is said that: if a child lives with criticism, he/she learns to condemn. If a child lives with hostility, he/she learns to fight. If a child lives with ridicule, he/she learns to be shy. If a child lives with shame, he/she learns to feel guilty. If a child lives with tolerance, he/she learns to be patient. If a child lives with encouragement, he/she learns confidence. If a child lives with praise, he/she learns to appreciate. If a child lives with fairness, he/she learns justice. If a child lives with security, he/she learns to have faith. If a child lives with approval, he/she learns to love himself/herself. If a child lives with acceptance and friendship, he/she learns to find love in the world.

In most of our towns children are running homes and taking care of fellow children due to the ravages of HIV/AIDs. Poverty has also revealed a dark side of our society with children being sent by parents and guardians to sell their bodies in order to feed the family. Such happenings bring shame to our nation and should be fought against at all costs. There are many NGO's that fight for the plight of the poor yet our streets are still infested with children living in poverty. Every Christmas festive season is the time for all stake holders to reflect and plan on how they are going to save the Zambian child from all these vices that rob him/her of his/her childhood and dignity.

Those who have the privilege of working with children do know that there is great potential in our children to emerge as better and productive citizens. Every time we approach Christmas, the festive season in many of our Churches and institutions let children be given chance to express themselves by speaking for themselves and educate society on their plight. We can learn a lot from our children if we are humble enough to give them a chance to teach us.

Every time we prepare to celebrate the birth of the Child Jesus we think and remember all the children of our world and do something about their plight. It is time for us all to show love and to bring joy to our children. For those children who have lost everything and are burdened by the cares of this world may they find the birth of the Child Jesus as a source of hope and may the child Jesus be identified in them. Jesus taught that the kingdom of God is full of those who are like little children.

As we rejoice and celebrate the birth of Jesus we remember that Jesus is present and comes to us every time in the many children we live with and encounter in the realities of our day to day events. Let us realize during this year's Christmas that the Jesus we encounter each day of our lives is a symbol of contradiction; one that has potential for a bright future and another that does not have a place to call home. May every Christmas be an opportune moment for us to give hope to the many children who have lost their parents and have no one to care for them. Many the energy, creativity and innocence of the children of the world teach us humility to be there for our children so as to guarantee them a safe and prosperous future where they can experience the love of the baby Jesus.

Work Referenced in this book

Ake, C. (1996) *Democracy and Development in Africa* (Washington, D.C.: R.R. Donnelley and Sons Co.

Ake, C. (1987). *Journal of Democracy: Rethinking Africa*. Vol. 2, No. 1, winter 1991.

Bacon, F.(2003) *Advancement of Learning.* In: *The Works of Francis Bacon,* Spedding and Ellis, eds. London: Longman, 1857–1870; Bartleby.com, 2010. www.bartleby.com/193/. [05th October].

Bacon, F.(2013) *The Advancement of Learning.* In *Squashed Philosophers.* In The Squashed Philosophers, Hughes, Glyn, ed. 2011. http://squapo.com/bacon.htm [30th September].

Benedict XVI.(2009). Encyclical Letter *Caritas in Veritate* (Charity in Truth: On Integral Human Development) Limuru: Paulines.

Bratton, M. "Zambia Starts Over," *Journal of*

Briggs, C. K. & Myers B. (1998). *MBTI: Self-Scorable.* California: CPP

Brown, Raymond and others, (1990), "The Parable of the Talents" in The New Jerome Biblical Commentary (New Jersey: Midas).

Callaghan, B. (2010). "Scandal and Scandals" [Available Online] On Thinking Faith: The Online Journal of the British Jesuits @www.thinkingfaith.org (Accessed: 16th May 2010).

Chishala, F (2006). "Camping in Room 13," [unpublished].

Davidson, R. (April 1992). *The Picador Book of Democracy.* Vol. 3, No. 2 Michigan: University of Michigan.

Elsner, J. and Rubies, J.(2002). (Ed). "Explanation,"(Paper presented at

Flusse, D. (1989), "Aesop's Miser/Parable of the Talents," in Thoma, Clemens and Wyschogrod, Michael (Eds), Parables and Story in Judaism and Christianity (NY:Paulist Press).Pg.9-25.

Fox J. (2006). "Zimbabwe's wild side," [Unpublished].

Fox, J. (2006). "Doubling the wintry capes," [Unpublished].

Gallagher, D. (2006). Journal for Christian Theology Research 10. Pgs, 39-63.

Gallup Strengths Finder. (2012). *Insight and Action-Planning Guide*. Gallup, Inc.

Hall, S. et al. (1980). *Culture, Media, Language*. London: Hutchinson.

Hartsock, J. (1997). "Introduction" in *A History of America Literary Journalism: The Emergence of a Modern Narrative Form*, Amherst: University of Massachusetts.

Hunter, A. (1960), *Interpreting the Parables*, S.C.M. Press, LTD.

Ihonvbere, J. O. (2002) *Economic Crisis, Civic Society, and Democratization* Asmara: Africa World Press, Inc. Inc.

Karl and Schmitter. (Summer 1991). "What Democracy Is...And Is Not," *Journal of Democracy*. Vol. 2, No. 3.

Kelly, M. J. (1991). *Education in a Declining Economy: The Case of Zambia. 1975-1985* Washington, D.C.: 1818 H Street.

Kennedy, G. (1994). *A New History of Classical Rhetoric*, NJ: Princetown University Press.

Kenneth, K. (1974). *Humanism in Zambia and a Guide to its Implementation: Part II*, Lusaka: Division of National Guidance.

Lehman, D. (2000). "Nonfiction Narrative and the Problem of Truth" in *Matters of Fact: Reading Non-fiction Narrative over the Edge*, Columbus: Ohio State University Press.

Matthews, Peter. (1996). "The Battle of Algiers: Bombs and Boomerangs" in *The Battles of Algiers*.

Meebelo, H. (1973). *Main Currents of Zambian Humanism Thought*. Lusaka: Oxford University Press.

Mofokeng, T (1992). "Hermeneutical Explorations for Black Christology," in Parkee, J (ed). *Exploring Afro-Christology*. Frarkfurt: Peter Larg.

Paul VI, (26 March 1967). Encyclical Letter, *Populorum Progressio*

Perkins, Pheme, (1981), *Hearing the Parables of Jesus* (NY: Paulist Press).

Phan, P (1996). "Jesus the Christ with an Asian Face," in *Theological Studies, 57*.

Quigley, B. (2013). "Identification as a Key Term in Kenneth Burke's Rhetorical Theory." On http://www.acjournal.org/journal/vol1/iss3/burke/Quigley.html (15.10.2013). [Online].

Reid, Dave, (1986), "Entrepreneurs for Christ" on *eDevotions for Growing Christians* [Accessed on 23rd October 2010 @ www.growingchristians.org/dfgc/enterpre.htm

Schiappa, E. (1999). "A Rhetoric of Motives." On *Outlines of Kenneth Burke's Writings,* @ http://www.umn.edu/burke/ROM.html (15.10.2013). Communication Department Studies. Minneapolis: University of Minnesota. [Online].

Severin, J. W. and Tankard J. (2001). *Communication Theories: Origins, Methods, and Uses in the Mass Media,* 5th ed. NY: Addison Wesley Longman, Inc.

Shankman, L. M, Allen J. S & Facca M. T. (2010). *Emotionally Intelligent Leadership for Students: Inventory.* Jossey-Bass.

Sichone and Chikulo. (1996). (Eds). *Democracy in Zambia: Challenges for the Third Republic,* Harare: Shapes Books.

Stein, Robert, (1981), *An Introduction to the Parables of Jesus,* Philadelphia: The Westminster Press.

Stein. J.(Ed),(1968)*The Random House College Dictionary,* Revised Edition, New York: Random House, Inc.

Theroux, P. (2002). "Blue Train Blues," in *Dark Star Safari: Overland from Cairo to Cape Town.* London: Penguin Books, 491-495.

Theroux, P. (2002). "The Trans-Karoo Express to Cape Town" in *Dark Star Safari: Overland from Cairo to Cape Town.* London: Penguin Books, 459 – 490.

Thomas, W. K. and Kilmann, H. R. (2007). *Thomas-Kilmann: Conflict Mode Instruments.* California: CPP Inc.

Thubron, C. "Writers Talk" (Video).

Velleman, D. (1999). "Narrative Visions," London: Reaktion.

Whetten, D. and Cameron K. (2011). *Developing Management Skills,* 8th ed. University of Michigan.

Zinkuratire, Victor and Colacrai, Angelo, (2007), *The African Bible,* Nairobi: Paulines Publication.

Made in United States
North Haven, CT
09 February 2022